*To Chuck and Julie,
my brother and sister.*

*Thank you for supporting your horse-crazy sister
and her dreams all these years.*

*I love you both with all my heart.*

# ACKNOWLEDGMENTS

*To God.* Thank You for giving me incredible adventures while holding me safely in the palm of Your hand.

*To Cindy and Kim, Jeanne and Doug, Joan and Gene, Mom and Dad.* May God bless you abundantly for all the hours you've encouraged and prayed for me and this book. Thank you.

*To Czar, my faithful and most trusted horse.* You were a priceless gift from God and are permanently etched into my heart.

*To Cindy Peterson, Dena Hooker, Shirley Rorvik, Jane Latus Emmert, Betsy Capon, Tricia Goyer, and Kathy Lamping.* I wouldn't be here without your unconditional love and support. There's a special place in my heart for all of you.

*To all my cowboy friends.* Thanks for taking this greenhorn under your wings.

*To Barbara Nicolosi-Harrington.* Your passion for teaching story has fueled hundreds of us to write for Christ. You're my writing hero. May the blessings of God abide with you.

*To Dennis Foley.* You're a fabulous writing teacher whose words inspire me. Thank you for investing thousands of hours in the "Authors of the Flathead."

*To Harvest House Publishers.* It's an honor to be part of your family.

*To Barbara Gordon, a kindred spirit.* You are a fabulous editor, and I'm looking forward to riding horses with you (and canoeing too).

*To Tom Fox, my daytime boss.* Thank you for giving me the opportunity to work for you.

*To Janet Kobobel Grant, my literary agent.* Your leadership is incredible. Thank you.

*To all the horses, mules, and dogs who have shared my life.* You have been my faithful companions and best friends.

# Contents

# A Note to You

*As they were walking along and talking together,*
*suddenly a chariot of fire and horses of fire appeared*
*and separated the two of them, and*
*Elijah went up to heaven in a whirlwind.*

2 KINGS 2:11

My heart pounds when I think about supernatural horses of fire majestically racing with a chariot of fire. Someday I'd like to meet those heavenly horses. And yet I feel that over the years I've had the opportunity to work with hundreds of heavenly horses and mules. These stories are my personal experiences, most of which took place during the 15 years I worked in the Bob Marshall Wilderness Complex in Montana. During this time God blessed me with very special friends, several exceptional horses to ride, and four fabulous dogs. I'm excited about sharing with you what they taught me about having a personal relationship with God and living for Christ.

I pray you'll adapt the wisdom I've learned to your life—to help empower you to experience a life richly blessed by God. Saddle up with me and ride through these pages for some exciting adventures!

*Rebecca*

1

# The Forge

*This third I will bring into the fire; I will refine*
*them like silver and test them like gold.*

ZECHARIAH 13:9

Billowy clouds drifted on a light breeze across the powder-blue Montana sky. My farrier's pickup and white trailer containing his shoeing supplies were parked on the dirt driveway by the barn. I leaned against the back of the metal trailer, holding SkySong's lead rope while he rested his head on Brian's chest. The powerful dapple gray-and-white gelding closed his eyes as Brian stroked his forehead. For a few moments the two of them stood quietly. Brian gently scratched SkySong's neck and under his breath asked him, "Are you ready to try something new? It's going to build your confidence."

Brian's green eyes twinkled when he turned to me and said, "I'd like to hot shoe SkySong today. I think it'll help him face some fears."

I tipped my head and ran my eyes over SkySong. I'd never seen a farrier use a forge to heat the steel horseshoes for a custom fit. I was curious to watch the process but was apprehensive about doing it with SkySong. He was young, and I was in the first stages of training him. I knew the noise of the blower on the propane-fueled forge would frighten him. I frowned as I thought of his timid character.

He was sure all new things contained a bogeyman. And that bogeyman had fangs dripping with blood and wanted to eat him. I inhaled a deep breath.

Brian grinned, "He needs to be stretched...challenged." He patted SkySong's forehead. "He'll do fine." He reached into his enclosed work trailer and lit the forge.

I never imagined that I would be the one who was changed by the forge.

With skillful hands, Brian trimmed and shaped SkySong's hooves. Stepping into the trailer, he glanced at SkySong. "This is going to sound pretty scary." Turning, he reached toward the forge and flipped on the blower.

*Whoosh!* It sounded like a small jet engine blasting air.

SkySong's eyes bugged out. Every muscle rippled tight. His neck arched. He shifted his weight backward. He braced his front legs, staring at the forge and looking like he was going to bolt at any second.

Lightly I rested my hand on his neck, wondering, *Does he have the fortitude to stay with us? Or will he bolt and become more fearful?*

The steel shoes on the rack clanked together as Brian lifted one off and meandered to SkySong's left shoulder. Lifting the hoof, Brian set the cold shoe on it, eyeing the shape to see what it needed to become.

SkySong focused on the bellowing forge. The whites of his eyes showed. The pulse in his throat pounded. His fear was so intense that it seeped into me. It was as if I was looking through eyes of fear—fear, a feeling I knew all too well—the haunting fears that I would make a horrible mistake, or the wrong decision, or even alienate myself from God. I rubbed my forehead. The only way SkySong could become free of his fears was to face them. *Will he do it or will he run?*

Brian stepped into the trailer, grasped the shoe with heavy-duty tongs, and held it inside the growling forge. When he withdrew it, heat waves danced off the glowing, reddish-orange metal. Watching SkySong out of the corner of his eye, Brian set the horseshoe on the anvil, picked up the hammer, and slammed it against the shoe. The hammer rang against the steel. He paused.

SkySong's head swung up. His nostril's flared. Wide-eyed he stepped back.

The hammer sang. SkySong shuddered with each blow. Sweat beaded behind his ears and dripped down his neck.

Brian dropped the shoe into the "slack tub" containing water. The shoe fizzed. Grabbing it with tongs, Brian pulled out the cooled shoe and strolled next to SkySong's shoulder, lifted the foot, and set the shoe in place. "Almost," he said.

I cringed as Brian thrust the metal back into the blasting forge. Then I watched the most amazing thing. Although the blower on the forge still sounded like a jet engine, SkySong now watched Brian out of curiosity instead of fear. This time when he set the red-hot shoe on the anvil and the hammer rang with each blow, SkySong lowered his head. Stroking his neck, I watched the muscles in his body ripple as they relaxed. I could almost see his mind at work: *This scary thing has happened before and it didn't hurt, so it must be okay.*

I wound a strand of his black mane around my finger. Brian wasn't just forging steel. With each blow he was forging SkySong's character with more confidence.

As I watched Brian's powerful arm wield the hammer, it was as if in the recesses of my mind I was watching God fashion the cold steel of my life. When I give my insecurities and fears to God, He puts them into His forge and heats them with His love until they are malleable. Then He creates confidence and trust. He takes my shortcomings and mistakes, and with artistic hands skillfully molds and shapes them into a valuable life. His forge isn't something to be feared or dreaded. It's where I become empowered. In the fire of His presence, He gives me the strength to go on.

While Brian continued to work with SkySong, I was lost in my reflections of God's forge, marveling that the God who created the universe loved me so much that He personally tailored an armored suit of His love to protect me—enabling me to stand in the face of my fears and conquer them.

> *Lord, thank You for revealing to me that Your forge isn't a place to hurt me; instead, it's a place where Your glowing love encompasses me. Amen.*

# 2

# Tag, Minnesota, Belgian

*Out of the ground the LORD God formed
every beast of the field and every bird of the
air, and brought them to Adam to see what he
would call them. And whatever Adam called
each living creature, that was its name.*

GENESIS 2:19 NKJV

The warm, spring sun glistened off the snow on the Rocky Mountain peaks, melting the snowpack and sending it trickling down the slopes. The drops of water woke up the hillsides after a long winter. Delicate yellow glacier lilies sprung up between nubbins of green grass. The frozen creeks were gently thawing, forming rivulets that skipped over mossy stones and sprayed a fine mist over the lacy ferns that lined the banks. Purple shooting stars nodded their heads in the breeze. The smaller creeks tumbled into the river named Rock Creek, which meandered through the narrow valley and close to the small ranch where I worked.

Squirrels chattered from the tops of the lodgepole pines. The heat of the sun warmed my back as I stood on the tailgate of the gold Ford pickup eyeing a tall stack of riding saddles that leaned against the cab. The truck was backed next to the side door of a tack trailer.

I lifted a saddle off the stack and lugged it through the door. Slinging it onto a saddle rack, I sighed. Sweat trickled down my back. I
tucked my thumbs into the pockets in my blue jeans and leaned in
the doorway. It had been a long day arranging the tack in the trailer.
I felt scruffy from doing the heavy lifting. I was dirty, tired, and ready
for a shower.

Gravel crunched under Larry's cowboy boots as he walked over.
He unzipped his brown vest and tossed it into the cab. "When you're
done, grab the pen and the notebook off the front seat and meet me
at the corrals. We're going to name the stock."

I nodded as he turned to go. Reaching for another saddle I wondered, *Name the stock? I can't tell them apart.* A couple days ago I'd
accepted a job working for Larry. He was an outfitter who took guests
on horse pack trips into the Bob Marshall Wilderness of Montana.
He'd recently purchased a semitruckload of stock: 1 horse and 19 mules.
The day he unloaded them, they all barreled down the ramp snorting
and blowing, bucking and kicking—and they hadn't stopped since.
I'd never seen a real live mule before. They all looked the same to me:
long ears, four legs, and a tail, although I did note some were black
and others were red.

I finished hauling the saddles into the tack trailer, grabbed the pen
and notepad, and then headed over to the corral.

Larry leaned on the top rail. "I'm going to have you write down
the names along with descriptions. Let's start with the horse."

I rested the notepad on a weathered wooden rail and wrote "horse."
She was easy. She looked like a horse: a cinnamon-and-sugar-colored
appaloosa mare with a stub of a tail that was nearly bald.

Larry looked her over. "Let's call her Melinda."

I wrote it down.

Larry rubbed his brown beard and pointed. "What do you think
we should call that black one?"

I looked in the direction he pointed and saw a half-dozen black
mules. "Which black mule?"

He waved his finger. "The gangly black mule. He's narrow-chested and has a creamy tan patch over his left eye—like a pirate's eye patch."

I giggled when I spotted him.

"Or maybe it's like a price tag. Let's call him 'Tag.'"

I scribbled "Tag, gangly black with price tag."

Larry leaned his head to the side, glancing through the herd. "What should we name that black one?" He glanced at me.

I stretched up, looking.

He waved his arm to the side. "Medium height and build with a white nose and white under its belly."

*White?* I frowned. I hadn't noticed the white on him. He looked like he'd dipped his nose halfway to his eyes in a bucket of milk.

Larry chewed on his lip. "Let's call him Minnesota."

Scrawling "Minnesota," I chuckled. My thoughts drifted to the story of creation in the Bible, when God created the animals and brought them to Adam. *What was it like having the Creator of the universe sit by your side as He paraded His creation before you, giving you the honor of naming them?* Did God sit in delight while He watched Adam gawk at the hopping kangaroos? Did Adam laugh at the long neck of the giraffe? Did God have the elephant blow his trumpety-trunk? A strange thought drifted through my mind. *God didn't stop creating when He finished the Garden of Eden.* My thoughts turned inward. *I wonder what God was thinking when He created me in my mother's womb? Did He delight when He formed me? Did He say, "I'm going to put a passion for horses in her so I'll give her long legs. And how about blue-green eyes that will change color according to what she wears"? Did He chuckle when He thought, "Her mother's Norwegian. I'll give her a small, ski-jump nose."* I smiled and brushed a tear from the corner of my eye. I'd never thought about God having fun creating me.

Even though I was sweaty and dirty, I stood a little taller and brushed a straggly strand of hair behind my ear. Eyeing the herd, I now saw them differently. One of the red mules was pudgy and short, another had a black mane and tail. I pointed to a chunky reddish one with a blond mane and tail. "That one looks like it's out of a Belgian draft horse. Can we name him 'Belgian'?"

Larry nodded.

*Lord, I'm glad I don't have to look special to be special in Your eyes. Amen.*

# 3

# 20 Wild-eyed Buggers

*He must believe and not doubt, because*
*he who doubts is like a wave of the*
*sea, blown and tossed by the wind.*

James 1:6

The April clouds hung below the mountain peaks and oozed a misty drizzle. Pulling the wool scarf tighter around my neck, I shut out the cold breeze. I leaned my elbows over the top of the wooden corral gate. Kai, my black-and-silver German shepherd, flopped down on some tufts of brilliant-green grass. I inhaled its fresh scent. *What could be better than spring in the Rockies?*

Nineteen head of dripping-wet mules and one horse milled in the mud. The wooden gate groaned as I pushed it open and slipped through. Before I could latch it, all the stock stampeded into the far corner. They squealed and shoved against each other, trying to get as far away from me as they could. I rolled my eyes and growled, "Spring in the Rockies would be perfect if these blasted critters would let me catch them!"

Draping the halter and lead rope over my shoulder, I glanced through the herd and eyed a black mule. The horse and mules froze in place with their necks arched, nostrils flared, and eyes wide. They seemed to hold their breaths as they watched me stroll toward them.

As soon as I stepped to the left, that black mule, along with some others, thundered across the corral. I squinted at him. *Blast!*

Squeezing my fingers around the lead rope, I lowered my voice. "Who is going to be the first catch of the day?" I singsonged. I scanned the bunch in front of me. A bay mule glanced over her shoulder. As soon as I took a step, she and a few others pivoted and ran around behind me. "You little buggers!" I muttered before clenching my teeth.

The day was turning out rotten—just like yesterday. At daybreak I had started catching stock and tying each one to a tree so they'd get used to being handled and tied up. I hadn't caught the last one until dusk—just in time to put them back into the pen for the night.

*Why did I take this job?* I groused. When my boss hired me, I thought God had given me my dream job. But I'd gotten kicked, bit, and dragged through the mud. *Maybe I should quit and look for another job?* I'd moved to Montana two weeks ago. I'd grown up in the cornfields of Minnesota, and after a couple years of college I'd gone to the Washington, DC, area, chasing the excitement of the city lights. As the novelty of the big city wore off, I found myself longing for the Montana mountains. Their majestic peaks glistened in my childhood memories of visiting there.

My brother Chuck was living in Missoula, Montana. I called him, stuffed my little car with everything I owned, and headed West. Kai, my German shepherd, perched in the passenger seat as the miles rolled past. When we arrived in Montana, we slept on Chuck's floor and I hunted for work. Jobs were tough to find. After some soul searching and much prayer, God led me to this place. In a month-and-a-half time frame, I had 1 horse and 19 mules to gentle and train to be saddled. But there were two problems: they were wild and hadn't seen too many humans and I hadn't ever seen a real live mule.

I took off my black cowboy hat and slapped it against my leg. Droplets of rain sprayed off. I whined, "This isn't any fun. Maybe I could wait tables until something else comes along." A dozen critters stood facing me. *How about the brown mule dead center?* I slid my boot forward. A few mules broke and ran, the brown one traipsing behind and waving her nose in the air. I groaned as I watched her snub me. She rolled past like a steam engine. Those critters were playing "Keep Away from Rebecca." Worse yet, I think they were enjoying themselves. *This is more like a nightmare than a dream. Even working at a fast-food joint would be better than this!*

Now only a cinnamon-and-sugar-colored mare and one mule stood in the corner. I glanced from the mare to the mule and then back again. The mule shifted his weight to run. I bounded toward him. The mare spun. She hammered me with her shoulder and sent me flying. They thundered by as I hit the mud on my back. "Ouch!" *She came out of nowhere! I wasn't even trying to catch her. Why did she do that?* Then the answer bubbled up from within me: *Your mind's been wavering. But how could she know?* I wondered. I caught my breath as understanding came. I'd been switching my mind and doubting every time I met resistance. First I chose one mule to catch, and if he squirted past, I picked another.

I rolled over and pushed myself up. Mud oozed between my fingers. My slicker and jeans were plastered to my body. Picking up the halter, I slung it over my shoulder. *How do I catch the one I want?*

The horse and mules snorted from the corner as I sauntered toward them. The cinnamon-and-sugar-colored mare stood toward the back. Our eyes locked. *You're it.* I stood still. A strange thought came to me: *Allow some to drift out of the corner.*

Slowly I walked 10 feet to my left, which was like opening up an invisible doorway. A few mules glanced at me and then at the wide spot. They roared past, bucking and kicking. I edged back to the center, closing the invisible gate. I grinned. *That worked! They didn't escape this time. I let them out of the corner.*

After a few moments, I walked 10 feet to the right, opening the invisible doorway again. A few mules skittered past. From then on, each time I opened a wide spot, some slowly drifted past. They had figured out the game.

The mare was the last one standing in the corner. Her nostrils flared and her eyes darted from me to the mules. I wiggled the toe of my boot in the mud and acted like I was ignoring her. Then I casually looked at her and softly said, "It's your turn." Slowly her head lowered. I stepped toward her and held out the back of my hand. Craning her neck forward, she sniffed, taking in my scent. I stepped closer and gently looped the lead rope over her neck. I slipped the halter over her nose and ears. Buckling it, I breathed a sigh of relief. *This is a snap.* All it took was for me to decide which one I was going to catch and then follow through on it. *Like this job,* I thought. *God led me here. Now it's up to me to apply myself and make it work.*

Over the next several days the stock quit bunching in the corner when I walked through the wooden gate. Instead, they watched to see which critter I wanted. The "Keep Away from Rebecca" game turned into "Keep Away from the One Rebecca Wants." There were still days when I got kicked, run over, and dragged through the mud, but I stuck with the job until it was done.

*Lord, help me to quit doubting and be more single-minded toward You in my everyday life. Amen.*

# 4

# Homesick No More

*From one man he made every nation of men,*
*that they should inhabit the whole earth; and*
*he determined the times set for them and*
*the exact places where they should live.*

ACTS 17:26

The door latched behind me, and the wooden porch steps squeaked as I walked and sipped my steaming cup of coffee. Gravel crunched under my boots as I strolled toward the pasture. A chickadee whistled its morning song, which drifted to me on the cool breeze. I turned up the collar on my prickly wool jacket as I gazed in awe at the beauty around me. Dawn's early light glowed from the snowy mountain peaks. The powder-blue sky was delicately laced with ribbons of wispy clouds splashed pink from the sunrise. Frost glittered from tufts of spring grass.

I buttoned the tan herringbone jacket and leaned my arms over the wooden corral gate, listening to the horses and mules munch hay. A wave of peace washed over me. It was the first time in my life that I felt like I was home. *How strange,* I thought. I'd moved to Montana only a few weeks ago. Every place I'd lived before this I'd felt unsettled and restless. There had been a longing in my being that was never satisfied. But since I'd arrived here, that craving had disappeared. I felt as if God had made this spot in the mountains for me. *Did God artistically create a place on earth for me?*

Melinda, the cinnamon-and-sugar-colored appaloosa mare with a rat tail, stopped chewing and looked up. With a few strands of hay hanging out one side of her mouth, she sauntered over to the gate and pushed her face toward me, begging for a rub. With my fingernails, I scratched behind her chin. She closed her eyes and leaned into my fingers. My mind drifted through the tidbits I knew about God. Before I was conceived, He'd planned the time frame of my birth and the purpose for my life. *Of course He loves me so much that He planned a place for me to live,* I decided.

Melinda pushed her head into my fingers and sighed. So did I. In the past, the longing in my heart had been homesickness for the place God had created for me. And now I stood in the right spot on earth, my heart fulfilled. *I'm going to stay here, in western Montana, wrapped in God's arms of love.*

*Lord, thank You for revealing the depths of Your love for me. Amen.*

5

# Nugget

*He paws fiercely, rejoicing in his strength
and charges into the fray.*

JOB 39:21

M y cowboy hat prickled against my forehead. I slipped it off and
wiped the sweat from my brow with my red bandana. I glanced
up at the sun. *It's already midday, and I've got to get these horses to the
trailhead and then drive back here tonight. I hope I can get them all in this
load.* Dusty's hooves drummed against the wooden ramp as I led him
into the back of the stock truck where six horses already stood tied. I'd
loaded them crosswise, tying the first one's head to the right side and
the second's to the left. When they rode sideways, nose to tail, they
didn't fight while was I driving down the road.

I tied the brown gelding in place and pushed against his side. "Scoot
over, Dusty. We still have to fit in Nugget." Dusty leaned against the
horse next to him. The truck rocked as each horse shifted a few inches
toward the front. I looked at the two foot space between Dusty and
the back wall of the truck and then gently slapped Dusty's side. "Nugget's not that skinny," I commented. The truck rocked some more but
there still was only two feet of space. I groaned. *I don't want to make
another trip for one horse—that would take hours and cut into my sleep
tonight.* Seven was the most horses I'd ever been able to load in the

truck. It wasn't because there wasn't enough room. One more *would* fit *if* I could get the horses to squeeze together. But they refused to cooperate.

I walked down the three-foot-wide ramp while sizing up Nugget, who was tied to the hitching rail. The boss had just bought him, so I didn't know much about his personality. He seemed to be a gentle giant. He was a deep, golden-brown with a reddish-brown mane and tail. Although he was tall, he didn't look it because he was built like a barn, with muscles that bulged in his chest and through his haunches. *There's no way that monster is going to fit in the truck.* I chewed on my cheek as I glanced in the back of the truck. *It wouldn't hurt to try,* I decided. *It's better than making another trip.*

Untying Nugget's lead rope I rubbed the cowlick on his forehead. "It doesn't look like there's room, but I need you to load in that truck, okay?" He looked at me with his kind, dark-brown eyes and batted his reddish-brown eyelashes.

The wooden ramp squealed in protest under the horse's weight as I led him up. By the time we got to the top, Dusty had moved toward the ramp. There wasn't even a crack for Nugget to wiggle into now. I tapped Dusty's side. "Move over!" I commanded. He braced all four feet and refused to budge.

I reached into the truck to tap Dusty again just as Nugget butted my rear with his nose, as if to move me out of the way. Turning toward him, I asked, "What do you…"

With his head, Nugget gently pushed me to the side of the ramp and stepped into the truck. With what looked like very little effort, he shifted around to stand in the proper place, bulldozing into Dusty, who stiffened like a board but was pushed sideways. The whites of Dusty's eyes showed, but he didn't put up a fight as he shifted his feet toward the front of the truck to keep his balance. Dusty bumped the next horse, who shifted and bumped the next one, and on down the line it went. Hooves grated across the wooden floor as all seven horses skidded to the front. After Nugget compacted them, he relaxed in the newly created wide spot and waited for me to tie him into place. I would've sworn he had a smile on his face!

I stood in awe, rubbing his neck. "You were terrific! I've never seen anything like that. And it looked like you had fun." I'd never thought of horses being buff or proud of their strength, but it was almost as if that gentle giant was created to flex his muscles and push his weight around. In all the years I knew him, he never acted vicious or mean, but if I ever needed to load an extra horse in the truck, I always saved Nugget for last.

*Lord, thanks for making superheroes in horses too. Amen.*

# 6

# On Patrol

*Godly sorrow brings repentance that leads to
salvation and leaves no regret, but
worldly sorrow brings death.*

2 Corinthians 7:10

A low, foggy mist hung above the valley floor. Thick gray clouds lay like a blanket above it, blocking the view of the mountains. It had rained so long that the spring air smelled damp like mushrooms. Wearing my long, yellow saddle slicker, I stood in the center of the muddy corral with a halter draped over my shoulder. After breakfast the boss would be trucking some of the horses to a different pasture, so I was catching them and tying them to the hitching rail by the tack shed.

I trudged across the corral toward Melinda, pulling my boots out of the mud with each step. Her appaloosa coat was soaked from the last several days of rain and dripped mud from where she'd lain on the ground last night. I buckled the halter around her head and turned toward the gate.

I expected to see Kai, my dog. He always sat at the gate, wagging his tail, waiting for me to catch the horses and mules. When I tied them to the hitching rail, he thought it was his job to guard them.

He'd trot in large circles around them like he was on patrol. But the spot where he always sat was empty.

I bowed my head. Droplets of water dripped from the rim of my cowboy hat. For a split second I'd forgotten that he was gone. I bit my cheek and closed my eyes. He'd died tragically last week, but that wasn't what haunted me. It was the circumstances surrounding his death that tore my heart to pieces.

While I tied Melinda to the hitching rail, my thoughts drifted back to the first day I'd seen Kai. I was living in Virginia and noticed an advertisement in the newspaper about puppies. For years I'd dreamed of having my very own dog. I drove to the farm in Maryland and instantly knew which of the pudgy puppies was mine—the one that waddled over and curled in my lap. The breeders said he was half German shepherd and half coyote. I thought, *Yeah, sure.* But as Kai grew he never barked, and his yips and howls proved his heritage.

Kai went everywhere with me—even to the grocery store. He wasn't just a dog; he'd become my most trusted companion. When we'd moved to Montana this past spring, I'd packed my little brown car and U-Haul. Kai jumped into the passenger seat and was my copilot as the mountains of Pennsylvania and the cornfields of Minnesota rolled past. *Now he's dead. I don't think I can forgive myself.*

With my wet gloves, I grabbed another halter off the ground and slogged back through the mud and into the corral. The horses and mules churned around me, not wanting to be caught. As they did, the mud became deeper. With each step I struggled to keep the black rubber irrigation boots on my feet. The horses and mules crowded into a corner. I crept closer, letting some animals sift out. A few mules made a mad dash, mud flinging from their hooves. A clump landed on my cheek. *Cold, like Kai's nose that last morning when he woke me up.*

I was lying on the floor of the bunkhouse snuggled in my brown sleeping bag. I vaguely remembered Kai's warm breath on my cheek. He lay with his head on his paws watching me with devotion, waiting for the alarm to buzz. As soon as it did, he stuck his cold, wet nose on my cheek to wake me up. I sat up and stretched. He licked my cheek, and I pushed him aside. "No licking my face," I ordered. But he wouldn't listen. It was like somebody had wound his spring one turn too tight.

When I didn't give him my full attention, he grabbed my socks and threw them into the air. I snatched them and grumped, "No! These are my socks." Then he wrestled with my boot. I hollered, "Kai, stop it! You're going to ruin my boot." I tried to grab it, but he played Keep Away. He bounded to the other side of the room and crouched down. When I tried to grab him, he ran full tilt across the room. After tackling him, I yelled, "Bad dog! You're a bad dog! I don't like you right now." He sulked onto his bed, and I went to the main house.

After breakfast I carried dishes to the sink and cleaned up the kitchen while the boss went out to load the horses into the trailer and take off.

The next thing I heard were his boots pounding up the wooden steps of the porch. The back door slammed open. His face was ashen. In shock he said, "When I drove out, Kai ran between the truck and the horse trailer." He took off his brown cowboy hat. "I never thought…" He exhaled. "The trailer tires ran over him and broke his back. I'm sorry…he's dead."

I turned away. Kai had gotten out, and I knew what he'd been doing. He was patrolling the horses, guarding them. Tears streamed down my face. *I should have made up with him before I came in and cooked breakfast. The last words he heard his master speak were, "Bad dog! I don't like you right now."* He was young. I never dreamed he'd die, and those words would hang in the air through eternity. *I'll never be able to forgive myself for those words.*

The cool morning breeze misted my face. Dusty stood in the corner behind a few black mules. Briefly my eyes caught his. "You're next, buddy." He hung his head and waited for me to halter him. We slurped through the mud to the hitching rail. My mind trailed up the mountain to where Kai was.

On that terrible day I took his body into the woods. With a pick-axe I dug a grave for him. Bitter tears of regret flowed down my face as I sat next to the hole. His brown, sightless eyes stared into the sky. I cradled his face in my hands. "You were the best dog I ever could have had. I loved you with all my heart. I wish you'd wag your tail, and I'd tell you that over and over." I kissed the top of his head, gently slid his body into the grave, and scooped rocks and dirt over him.

Wallowing in my grief, I tied up Dusty and grabbed another halter. The heavy corral gate groaned as I pushed it open and stepped almost knee-deep in the churned-up mud. The horses and mules bunched in the corner, squealing and trying to hide. Tucked in the very back was a bay Arabian mare named Dream. The mud latched onto my boots, and I curled my toes under and lifted my knees straight up to keep them on my feet.

Every other step I would wait for a few horses to shake out of the corner. Finally only Dream and a red mule stood facing me. Dream's nostrils flared, and her eyes darted back and forth. She broke to my left. I shifted my weight and tried to pick up my feet, but the deep mud held fast. My right foot slipped out of the boot. I held it high but lost my balance. I tried to put my stocking foot down to brace myself, but my long yellow slicker had wrapped around my legs. Holding out my hands, I fell facedown, my arms plunging almost elbow-deep into the mud.

I shoved myself to a standing position, shaking the goo from my arms. Mud oozed over the top of my sock. "Yuck." I reached down and pulled the boot out of the mud. "Now I've got to wash my leg." As soon as I said that, I heard deep inside of me, "That's not all you need to wash." I inhaled. I'd been emotionally exhausted this past week, sinking into the pit of despair, mired by the last words I'd spoken to Kai. No amount of wallowing in regret would open his grave. I couldn't change what had happened. Kai was dead.

Carrying the boot like it was a dead fish, I limped to the house, avoiding the sharp gravel with my stocking foot. I set the boot on the porch and hopped across the floor to the bathroom. After washing my leg in the tub, I leaned my hands on the sink. I was so filled with shame I couldn't look at myself in the mirror. Tears streamed down my face. "God, please forgive me for wallowing in my mistakes."

Guilt swirled through my mind. Inhaling a deep breath, I forced myself to look into the mirror at my bloodshot eyes. I swallowed hard. "Rebecca," I said as tears gushed down my face, "I forgive you." I gripped the cold marble sink and sobbed. Saying those words while looking directly into my eyes freed me from the chains of guilt. As the tears flowed, relief washed over me. Peace flooded my spirit.

Over the summer, the hurt of losing Kai gradually eased, but I've never forgotten what a special dog he was. He planted a valuable lesson in my heart: Sorrowing over things I can't change sucks me into a pit of despair and turns me away from God. The way to climb out is by asking God—and me—for forgiveness.

*Lord, when I'm hurting, lift me up in Your hands and hold me tight. Amen.*

# 7

# Identity Crisis

*In him we were also chosen, having been predestined*
*according to the plan of him who works out*
*everything in conformity with the purpose of his*
*will, in order that we, who were the first to hope*
*in Christ, might be for the praise of his glory.*

EPHESIANS 1:11-12

A warm, spring breeze rolled down the mountains. The rays of the morning sunlight danced through the pines. Melinda stood tied to the hitching rail. In the pasture behind her were 19 mules crowding the barbed-wire fence, longingly gazing at Melinda as if she were a dazzling movie star. I glanced at Melinda. She wasn't much to look at. Her tall, rawboned frame jutted with her angular shoulders and hips. A few straggly hairs stuck out of her salt-and-pepper-colored mane, and her tailbone was nearly bald. I patted her neck. "But your personality makes up for your looks."

I heaved the heavy western saddle onto Melinda's back. I was looking forward to some saddle time. I could think clearer from the saddle than anyplace else. I reached under Melinda's belly for the cinch. My job of gentling the mules was coming to an end in less than a week, and my boss already had a full crew lined out for his outfitting season. I'd been pounding the pavement in Missoula looking for a job.

I had several possibilities, but as far as figuring out what to do next, my life was a blur.

I pulled the cinch tight. Two mules squealed. I glanced up as one of the black mules in the back pushed its way through the crowd to the fence. Another mule nipped it in the rear. The war was on. They kicked and squealed, all vying for the spot on the fence line closest to Melinda. Worried they would get cut on the barbed wire, I hollered, "Hey, get away from the fence!" But they were so absorbed in their squabble that they either didn't hear me or chose to ignore me. I reached down, picked up a clod of dirt, and lobbed it at them, hitting the front mule in the chest. Stunned, they all scattered.

I shook my head. "Snuffy said you guys loved horses better than each other, but this is ridiculous!" I swung my leg over the saddle and reined Melinda down the driveway. Her fan club escorted us.

Snuffy, an old-time cowboy friend, had yarned many hours about mules. I relished his coaching because my time around mules was limited. He would lean back in his chair at the dinner table and brag on the critters. He'd shared that one of the reasons outfitters preferred mules over horses for backcountry work was that mules didn't need to be put inside a fence to hold them. He said that if you tied up the horses, you could turn the mules loose and they wouldn't leave the country. They stayed with the horses because they didn't care for the other mules.

I turned left out of the driveway and watched the crowd follow in the pasture. Melinda's hooves crunched on the gravel road. *Why do they dislike each other?* Mules are a hybrid animal. Over 90 percent of them are sterile, not able to breed. Mules are the product of a donkey dad and a horse mom. They usually were the best qualities of the horse and donkey rolled into one. They ate less, drank less, and the old saying "Stubborn as a mule" was true—but only because you couldn't get a mule to do anything they thought would hurt themselves. This made vet bills almost nonexistent for them.

My saddle creaked as I leaned back and glanced at their long ears and straight backs. *A hybrid…a freak of nature.* I snickered. *Did they know they were freaks?* The sun warmed my back, and I melted into the saddle. My thoughts roamed over the mule issue. *Born of a horse mom. That's it! When they were born, they imprinted on their moms! Each one thought it was a horse.* I chuckled. The mules' ears swiveled like periscopes as I jabbered, "So when you look at the other mules you see freaks. And you think you're nothing like them—after all, you're horses." How would they know they weren't horses? They didn't have any mirrors. I laughed as I thought of holding up a mirror in front of a mule.

The mules lined the fence as Melinda and I walked beyond the field and down the road. I wrapped my legs around her and nudged her into a trot. Her hooves clopped down the hard-packed road as we rounded a bend. My mind wandered. *So now that I've gotten the mules figured out, what am I going to do for work?* I'd applied at several restaurants. I'd been a waitress previously but didn't care for the grouchy, hungry customers. *But it would put beef and beans on my table.* The road passed between tan rock cliffs. *What else can I do?* After talking with a banker, I looked around at the women tellers, all wearing pantsuits and skirts. *I'm not much of a pantyhose-type gal.* Not that I wouldn't do it to get some cash flow, but it wasn't me.

Just yesterday I'd been offered a job as a pharmaceutical representative. The money was good, but the job required travel. I sighed. I'd moved to Montana because I wanted to live here. *I don't want to be gone all week—on the road, sleeping in motels, and eating in restaurants in other states.*

The forlorn sound of a mule braying drifted down the road, followed by a chorus of brays. I shook my head. *It must be hard going through life not knowing who you are, having an identity crisis every day.* A strange question drifted through my mind: *Am I any different than the mules?* I had no clue who I was. Here I sat in the saddle of my dream job, which was ending. I was pounding on doors of businesses in town looking for a job, when I really wanted work that involved horses. It didn't make sense.

As long as I could remember I'd had a passion for horses. I was sure God tucked that love of horses inside my heart. *Why am I looking for a job in town?* As the next few miles of gravel road passed under Melinda's hooves, I looked into the mirror of my life and saw clearly, perhaps for the first time, that I was a horse gal through and through. This was the first opportunity I'd had to do what I wanted with my life. And this job was the first time that I felt like I "fit in." Before this I'd always felt like the square peg in a round hole. A freak. All my growing up years I'd dreamed of having horses. It was my goal in life. *So why am I not looking for a job with horses?* By the time Melinda and I turned into the driveway, I'd made up my mind to look for horse jobs.

Strangely, just the next day the cook my boss had hired for the summer season quit. So Larry offered me the job! I would be working in the mountains within the Bob Marshall Wilderness Complex in some of the most pristine country in the world—from the saddle! It didn't take long for me to respond, "Yes!"

*Lord, please remind me to keep looking into the mirror of my life so I reflect who You created me to be. Amen.*

8

# Wandering Off

*Surely, O LORD, you bless the righteous; you
surround them with your favor as with a shield.*

PSALM 5:12

I pulled nine mules loaded with bales of hay up the winding trail.
My lanky, six-month-old German shepherd puppy skittered from
rocks to stumps, smelling and exploring. He disappeared around a
bend. "Cochise, stay close!" I hollered. He bounded back. Stopping
in front of my horse, he playfully dropped his front end, his rear in
the air wiggling, as if to say "Catch me if you can!" Then he ran full
blast up the trail and out of sight.

This was Cochise's first trip into the wilderness. Last spring Kai,
my German shepherd, had gotten killed before the season started. All
last summer, while I rode the trails, I longed to have a dog trotting
by my side. I knew my boss wasn't fond of dogs, but there was something deep inside me that needed one. I didn't feel complete without a
canine companion. So last winter, while I was working a town job, I'd
watched the classifieds and found a pudgy black-and-silver German
shepherd puppy. In May I prayed that God would soften my backcountry boss's heart and let me bring the pup on trips. When I asked
the boss, his lips tightened as he lectured me about dogs chasing deer,

spooking the mules, and causing "wrecks" (mule pileups). But he did agree to let me bring Cochise on a couple crew trips on a trial basis. If the puppy stayed with me and behaved, he would consider letting him come on more trips. If not, I'd have to give him away or look for another job. I looked at the empty trail in front of me and shook my head. *How am I going to keep Cochise from wandering off?*

Billowy gray clouds rolled overhead. I put my fingers together and whistled. Nothing. "Cochise!" I yelled. Silence…except for the sound of the pack string's hooves hitting the dirt and an occasional scolding squirrel. *Darn pup!* I turned around, checked the rocking loads on the mules to make sure they were riding balanced, and then nudged Amarillo, my copper-colored saddle horse, into a faster walk.

It was June and the outfit was in full swing. The crew was working as fast as they could in different locations to prepare for a busy season. One group fixed fence at the end-of-the-road camp and staging area, and another group worked 14 miles down the trail at Monture Camp stretching white canvas wall tents over wooden frames. Two of us were pulling round-trip hay runs, going back and forth between the two places. We'd leave the end-of-the-road site and ride into Monture Camp pulling nine head of mules loaded with hay. After unloading at the camp, we'd ride back out with the mules trailing us to get the next load.

I looked down at the mucky trail and could clearly see Cochise's tracks. *He's been running for miles and hasn't slowed up. He could be in Canada by now. If the boss finds out, we're toast.* "Cochise!" He rounded the bend, blasting toward me. I threw my hands into the air. "Where have you been? Stay close!" I ordered. Cochise stopped, watched me ride past, and then fell in behind the last mule.

Bright-yellow arnica flowers swayed in the cool breeze. I relaxed in the saddle as the miles rolled past. I turned and checked the mule loads. No Cochise. I hollered and whistled, but it was half an hour before he trotted up beside me. I wagged my finger and scolded, "Just where have you been? You don't know how serious this is. Stay close!"

He pumped his tail and trotted in front of me. But in less than a mile Cochise vanished. I fidgeted with the reins and fumed. *God, what am I going to do? The boss is never going to let this slide. But I want a dog.*

When I reached the fork in the trail to head up to Monture Camp, I couldn't see any tracks or my pup. But when I rode up to the hitching rail, Cochise was playing tag with D.J., a wrangler. I stepped out of the saddle and growled, "How long has he been here?"

D.J. rubbed his reddish-brown moustache and smiled. "Off and on all day."

I tipped back my black cowboy hat. "All day?"

"Yep. About every hour or so he shows up and plays and then disappears."

I tied Amarillo to the rail as my heart sank. Cochise had been running back and forth between me and Monture Camp. He wasn't being a bad dog; he was merely a puppy with boundless energy who loved to explore exciting new places and play with his friends. I shook my head. *This is not going to fly with the boss.*

The boys helped me unload the mules. Within an hour I pulled out of camp and headed back to the end-of-the-road area. Cochise trotted in front of me until my thoughts drifted…then he did too. When I arrived at end-of-the road, Cochise was playing with the crew. It was worse than I'd thought. Cochise had been running between me, Monture Camp, *and* end-of-the-road all day.

By the time we unsaddled the mules, turned them loose in the corrals, and jumped in the pickup, it was nine o'clock. We were exhausted and hungry for dinner, but Cochise wasn't anywhere to be found. I turned the key and the engine roared to life. *He's probably on his way back to hunting camp. I can't wait. I have to cook dinner and get some sleep.* Slowly I pulled out of the corral area and headed home. We watched for the pup but never did see him. Over dinner I avoided the boss, afraid he'd say something about Cochise, but he stayed aloof and quiet.

All night I tossed and turned. *What if the coyotes get Cochise? What if he wanders out of the country? What if I have to get another job?* But I was too exhausted to drive the half hour back to the corrals to check. *God, please take care of that pup. And could You make everything work out?*

Before daybreak I fried bacon, pancakes, and eggs for the crew's breakfast and packed sack lunches. My tummy churned as I thought about the pup. *Is he alive? Will he stay with me on the trail today? Will it be another disaster?* When I drove the truck into the corral area, I saw that black-and-silver pup perched next to the hitching rail where I'd tied Amarillo the night before. Cochise bounded to the truck and tackled me when I opened the door. He licked my face as I hugged him. I pushed him back and stared into his brown eyes. "You have got to stay with me. No nonsense today."

Cochise shadowed me as I haltered the mules. As soon as I tied Amarillo to the hitching rail, Cochise sat under Amarillo's belly, waiting. He stuck like glue the entire way to the hunting camp. He once again lay under Amarillo's belly while the mules were unloaded. When I slipped into the saddle to leave, Cochise stayed by Amarillo's side until the trail became too narrow. Then he moved back and trotted behind the end mule. For 14 miles Cochise never let me out of his sight. And he was the first one to jump into the pickup when we arrived at the end-of-the-road area.

As the pickup bumped down the dirt road toward home, I marveled at the change in Cochise. *Was it the scary night on the trail? His fear of losing me?* Whatever it was, I knew God's hand was in it.

That night as I snuggled into bed, Cochise stood next to me and rested his head on the mattress. His big, brown eyes softly looked into mine. He leaned into my fingers as I scratched behind his ears. "Well, boy, it looks like God worked everything out. The boss told me tonight that you get to come on the next trip."

The rest of Cochise's life, whenever we were at the end-of-the-road corral or on the trail, he stuck to me like Velcro. And since then there have been days when I needed God's favor. At those times I remember that wiggly black-and-silver German shepherd. I figure if God can change a six-month-old puppy and my boss's heart overnight, He can do anything.

> *Lord, thank You for treating me like I'm Your favorite daughter. Amen.*

9

# *Rockslide!*

*If you can help your neighbor now, don't say,*
*"Come back tomorrow, and then I'll help you."*

Proverbs 3:28 NLT

The horses and mules were tied to the pines, their rear ends turned into the wind as it howled through the trees and spit sleet. Four of us bundled in yellow saddle slickers huddled around the campfire. Sitting on the dead trees that we'd drug next to the fire, we propped our boots as close to the flames as possible to warm our toes. I swallowed the last bite of my peanut butter sandwich and watched my wet boots steam from the heat. Tipping my soggy black cowboy hat back a bit, I stared west, the direction the storm was coming from. Black billowy clouds stretched as far as I could see, promising bad weather for at least the rest of today and perhaps into tomorrow. I shivered and I rubbed my hands together over the dancing flames. *I hope I packed enough warm clothing.*

It was late June in the high country. Today was the second day of our seven-day outing. Planned as the first trip of the season, it was supposed to be crew time to explore new trails. At the last minute a guest called from Europe wanting to come on a horse pack trip. And this was the only time he could join us. I'd picked him up at the airport the day before yesterday and frowned when he claimed one

40

itty-bitty duffel bag as his luggage. *There's no way he packed everything that was on the suggested clothing list we sent him. That duffel is barely big enough for one change of clothes!*

I glanced across the fire at Alex. His short, blond bangs poked out from under the brim of his cowboy hat. The rosy cheeks of his baby face made him look much younger than his 22 years. He was watching his soaked, lightweight hiking boots steam. A trail of smoke encircled him. Standing up, he rubbed his arms and turned his back to the fire. Pivoting his slender frame, he warmed himself like a hotdog on a grill. *He must be frozen. He's not packing much meat on him. He couldn't have many warm clothes in that tiny bag.*

A thought bubbled up from my spirit: *Why don't you loan him a jacket and your extra pair of boots?* I cringed. My extra jacket and boots were in the pannier bags on the mule named Johnston. It wouldn't be hard to unbuckle the bags and dig them out. *But I only have one change of clothes, and I don't know if that'll be enough to keep me warm. What if the clothes I'm wearing get wet? Then what?* I stuffed the thought in the deep recesses of my mind as I snuggled next to the fire.

Larry, the boss, took off his brown cowboy hat and shook the water from it as he stood up. "We better douse this fire and put some miles on. We might run into snow before we get to camp tonight." After smothering the fire with water from the creek, we waded through the tall, wet grass to our horses. My jeans soaked up every drop.

Richard, the wrangler, tied three loaded pack mules together into a string while the rest of us tightened the cinches on our mounts. I untied Johnston and led her next to Sunrise, a palomino mare. After swiping the rain out of my saddle, I settled in. Richard nudged his brown mare into a mile-eating pace. The mules traipsed behind, followed by me leading Johnston, and then Alex, and then Larry at the tail end so he could chat with Alex.

The trail snaked up the mountain. The higher we rode, the colder the wind. I pulled up the collar on my slicker. In an hour we'd be riding under the lip of the 9000-foot peaks of the Continental Divide.

There could be a blizzard up there. I hunkered down in my saddle, trying to stay warm while the water in my jeans wicked into my socks. A drop trickled down into my boot. I shivered. *Alex could use your jacket and boots.* I whisked the prompting away with a dream of putting on a warm and dry pair of boots when we got to camp tonight.

Mile after mile we plodded. The exceptionally rainy spring had saturated the ground and nourished the forest. The new growth on the pines and the larch trees glowed lime green. Tall ferns lined the banks of the small streams that tumbled down the hillsides. Delicate purple shooting stars poked their faces between blades of grass, and hundreds of red indian paint brush dotted the hillsides between tall spires of white bear grass that nodded their heads in the breeze.

Horse and mule hooves clattered over rocks as we wound higher. The wind whined through pine boughs and some snowflakes floated past. The trail narrowed to the width of one horse and followed along the base of a rock wall on our left. To our right, the mountain sloped steeply, hundreds of feet down to a creek that overflowed its banks and roared down the mountain. I glanced around. Water ran everywhere. Even from the rocks above us miniature waterfalls cascaded and ran in rivulets on the trail, making it muddy and loosening the stones. The horses and mules sloshed rhythmically along.

I set the reins on Sunrise's neck as I rubbed my hands together, warming them inside my wet gloves. The thought prickled me again: *Alex is probably really cold. He could use your...* I drowned out the idea. *If he'd brought the clothes on the list he would be fine.*

Gathering the reins I looked up as we rounded a bend in the mountain. I felt the blood drain out of my face. Ahead the whole mountain turned into nothing more than a jumbled rockslide of shale. I chewed on my lip as I reviewed what I knew about shale. It could be extremely dangerous because it was a flat rock. If the trail was settled, we'd be okay because shale interlocks with the rocks around it creating a flat, solid surface. But if it's not, the flat faces will slide against other pieces and it's like riding on ice.

Richard reined in his horse, and the mules behind him stopped. Cinching down his tan cowboy hat, he turned in the saddle to look for direction from the boss. Sunrise stopped. As I turned to look over my shoulder, water poured off the rim of my cowboy hat, trickled down my yellow slicker, and dripped off my boot. My stomach churned as I glanced over the edge of the narrow trail and into the deep canyon.

Larry stood in his stirrups, appraising the faint trail and the steep slope. He yelled, "What do you think, Richard?"

Richard stroked his brown moustache. "Looks better than trying to turn around."

Larry settled in the saddle. "Okay, let's go. But spread out."

I gathered the reins. *Turn around? There isn't room to turn around.* Holding Sunrise back, I gave Richard and the mules about a 15-foot lead. Steel horseshoes clanged against the shale. My heart pounded as I nudged Sunrise forward. Slowly we all wound onto the shale. I chewed on my lip and focused on Richard. *Only 200 yards more...150...50...25...10 yards.* Suddenly the mountain churned. I stopped Sunrise and gasped. A panel of rocks under Richard and the three mules broke loose.

The mountain rumbled with the deafening sound of the shale shifting. The noise came across the cliffside like a wave. Richard grabbed his reins. His horse and the mules braced their feet as they slid sideways and down several feet. I caught my breath as the ground under Sunrise's hooves shook. I grabbed the saddle horn. With the next step, the shale underneath Sunrise broke loose. The ground churned and gave way. We slid sideways down the steep slope. Shale boiled around Sunrise's legs.

As suddenly as it started, it stopped. My heart raced. A few pieces of shale clattered to the bottom of the canyon. The whole world seemed deathly still. Sunrise's eyes bulged, her nostrils flared, and her body was as stiff as a board. I exhaled. My throat was tight and my mouth dry. Cold sweat covered my body.

Richard and the mules were only seven feet lower than where they'd started. It was about the same distance for me. I glanced behind me. Johnston's nostrils flared and her eyes were wide. Alex's face was white and his grip on the saddle horn tight. I knew the excessive water run-off from the wet spring had formed an underground river beneath this section of shale, washing away the dirt and loosening the rocks.

I held my breath as I watched Richard nudge his horse forward... one step...two steps...three steps...

The mountain groaned.

My heart pounded in my ears. I wanted to close my eyes but didn't dare. My stomach churned. I didn't want to nudge Sunrise forward, but I couldn't stay here either. I licked my dry lips. My hands shook as I held the reins and grabbed a clump of mane with my left hand. I had Johnston's lead rope in my right hand so I could toss it and not get tangled up in case the whole mountain cut loose.

My world narrowed to Sunrise and me. I took a deep breath and held it as I eased Sunrise forward. One step...two... I felt the rocks shift under Sunrise and cringed, trying hard not to gasp for breath.

The mountain rumbled and shook. Earth gave way and we fell a few more feet. My feet slammed into the stirrups as we stopped and my weight settled.

Rocks shifted beneath us. I clung to the saddle horn. Boulders crashed down the mountain. We skidded sideways, and Sunrise braced her legs. Waves of rocks clattered into the creek below. We finally stopped.

I swallowed hard. I didn't want to move because it might start the mountain shifting again. I was too scared to look over my shoulder to check on Johnston. I took a deep breath. My hand felt like a club as I patted Sunrise. My voice wavered as I said, "Not far to go." I felt the saddle rise as Sunrise took a deep breath too.

I tightened my grip on the saddle horn and clump of mane and gently squeezed my legs. Sunrise hesitantly raised her front right leg and carefully placed it on the shale. Easing inch by inch, we moved forward. Rocks shifted under her feet.

The mountain roared and vomited shale. The ground gave way. Rocks banged against my feet in the stirrups before clattering underneath us and down the mountainside.

Sunrise braced her feet. We skidded a few feet as waves of rocks washed past us. We stopped.

I rested Sunrise, and then we stepped forward again. We slid again. Finally Sunrise scrambled up the bank to solid footing. Johnston was right on our tail.

I reined Sunrise around so I could watch Larry and Alex. Each time the horses took a step, my tummy tightened and I grabbed the saddle horn. After everyone scrambled to safety, I gathered the reins and turned Sunrise down the trail. My whole body trembled.

Winding through the pines a half mile down the trail, we were greeted by a chorus of mules braying. We rode into a meadow where Richard stood warming his hands over a campfire. After tying Sunrise and Johnston to dripping wet trees, I strode to the crackling fire. Larry and Alex quietly filtered over. Each of us stood pale and silent next to the fire, warming our hands and mentally processing what had just happened. After a few minutes Richard stroked his moustache and said, "Well, that was interesting."

My mouth dropped open. I glanced at Larry and Alex, who stood speechless as well. Suddenly we erupted into laughter. All the tension from our harrowing adventure flowed out. We slapped each other on the back and tears rolled down our cheeks. We laughed until our guts hurt.

I held my stomach and looked at Richard. "You take one step, the whole mountain moves, and you call that 'interesting'?"

Richard shrugged. With the toe of his boot he shoved a burning log further into the fire.

The next half hour we snuggled next to the fire and watched the column of smoke. My body relaxed. A stick in the fire popped, shooting embers into the air. I glanced across the fire at Alex. His lips were pursed and held a tinge of blue as he rubbed his wet gloves together, trying to warm his hands. That still small voice said, *When you take one step in obedience toward Me, I'll move the* whole *mountain for you.*

I grimaced. I knew what that was about. God's Spirit had been urging me to loan Alex my extra jacket and boots, but I'd been ignoring Him. Those boots and jacket had become my security, and I didn't want to let loose. My heart felt heavy. I'd put more faith in my clothing than trusting my God and doing what He was asking me to do.

I kicked the toe of my boot into the dirt. "Hey, Alex, I've got an extra jacket and boots tucked in the panniers on Johnston. Would you like to use them?"

Alex's face brightened. "Are you sure you don't need them?"

I turned toward Johnston. "I'll be okay."

The boots and jacket fit Alex perfectly, and he used them the rest of the trip. That afternoon when I got chilly I walked and led Sunrise to warm up. The next day the skies cleared off and the sun came out.

I've never forgotten that harrowing ride or what happened when I gave what I had out of obedience to God. And He gave me something better—warm, sunny days!

*Lord, when You ask me to give, help me to do it willingly, knowing that You'll move the mountain when I take one step in obedience to You. Amen.*

# 10

# Who's Watching Me?

*[Jesus said,] "I am the bread of life."*

JOHN 6:48

The kitchen tarp billowed in the light breeze. I bent over and pulled a loaf of bread out of the wooden bread box and set it on the makeshift kitchen counter. Suddenly I got a creepy feeling—like somebody was watching me. I glanced behind me. Nothing. My eyes swept camp. While I cooked dinner, the guests were chattering and setting up their green tents. The crew was unsaddling the horses and mules, which were tied to the rope corral under the scraggly pines. I pushed back my bangs. *Weird.*

The plastic bag crackled as I untied the twisty and set the bread on the counter next to our dinner plates. Then I felt it again—that icky feeling. Quickly I spun around, eyeing the meadow. Only a trail of smoke from the wood cookstove curled over the grass. *Who would be way up here?* It was June, and I was on one of my first summer trips. The last two days we'd ridden the horses and packed all our gear on the mules through miles of rugged mountains.

The trail wound through canyons and over ridges. I'd ridden through country of which I'd dreamed about. At times we sat on the shoulder of a mountain, with the wind blowing in our faces, staring at the rows of snowcapped peaks that stretched as far as we could see. I was in awe of God's creation, and in my mind I talked with Him as I rode the trail. With every mile I felt like He was filling my spirit. Up, up, up we climbed until we pulled into this little shelf of a meadow that hung under the sheer rock wall of the Continental Divide. I felt like we were camped at the end of the world all by ourselves. *So who's watching me?* I wondered.

The door on the cookstove squealed as I opened it and tossed in a chunk of wood. It belched smoke as I closed it. I felt that yucky feeling again. Standing still, I glanced behind me. Something tan twitched. I held my breath and slowly turned. A deer stood frozen in place behind the tree that the kitchen tarp guyline was tied to. She wasn't 10 feet from me. I smiled. "Aren't you a pretty girl?" Her ears pivoted toward me.

The breeze flapped the blue kitchen tarp. We stood facing each other for a moment. Then she stretched her neck toward me. Her shiny wet nose wiggled as she sniffed. I chuckled. "Oh, I get it. You're begging for dinner. But I don't feed wild animals."

She turned sideways. Every line of her ribs showed, telling of the hard winter she'd endured. And her udder was filled with milk. I grimaced. "So you've got a hungry baby." Glancing through the kitchen, the bread bag caught my eye. Slowly I crept toward it and pulled out a heel. Ripping off a small piece, I tossed it toward her. She flinched. Her eyes stared at the bread. Dropping her nose to the ground, she strained her neck and snuffled. With her eyes glued to me, she craned her neck and grabbed the bread.

She chewed and smacked her lips. I smiled. "Do you want another piece?" I tossed another. Globs of winter hair hung from her coat. With compassion, I ripped off another bite and threw it. "Bread has all kinds of nourishment in it." Her eyes darted from the bread to me and then back to the bread. She stepped forward and gobbled a piece.

My heart felt warm as I watched her chew her cud. I knew that I was giving her much-needed nourishment to build up her skinny body. As I tossed her another chunk, a strange thought drifted through my mind: *Jesus…the Bread of Life.* Then I thought of how peaceful I felt riding the mountains with Him by my side. It was as if the time I invested with Him was nourishing my spirit the same way the crusts of bread were nourishing the doe's body. *I wonder if God feels the same compassion toward me when I invest time with Him?*

Over the next two days I tossed the bite-sized pieces so they landed closer and closer. By the time we pulled down camp and rode out of the valley, that doe was eating out of my hand and I was looking forward to riding thousands of miles with God by my side.

> *Lord, there's nothing like Your presence to nourish my hungry spirit. Amen.*

# 11

# Stinky Feet

*"No," Peter protested, "you will never ever*
*wash my feet!" Jesus replied, "Unless I*
*wash you, you won't belong to me."*

John 13:8 NLT

Lightning cracked and flashed across the afternoon sky. The wind swirled, snatching the napkins off the serving table and throwing them into the sky. The ground under my boots rumbled from the thunder. Suddenly the floodgates of heaven opened. Rain fell in sheets. It pounded the green kitchen tarp so hard I wondered if the ropes would break. I nestled in my camp chair by the wood cookstove, stirring the au gratin potatoes and flipping the ham steaks. I looked over at the second kitchen tarp. The guests huddled under it in the center, around the portable picnic tables, trying to stay away from the blowing rain. It was the fifth day of our 10-day summer pack trip. Every day—and night—it had poured. We were all tired, wet, and trying to be good sports. At least I was trying to *look* like a good sport.

The rain was the least of my grumbles. The trip was filled to the maximum with guests, so the main boss wanted to send someone along to help me in the kitchen. Only they couldn't find anybody with experience. Thinking they were helping me out, they sent Todd.

Todd had been raised as far away from the woods as a person could get. And I'm sure that wherever that was, no boys had been allowed in the kitchen.

From the moment we pulled the string of mules into the new camp-site, I had just over an hour to set up the kitchen and cook dinner for 15 people. I had to hustle. But not Todd. He moved at a snail's pace. And he had a knack of standing in the way. If that wasn't bad enough, he kept asking silly questions, like how did I want to have the carrots peeled. *I don't care. Just peel the blasted things!* I wanted to shout. He couldn't even find a good spot in the creek to draw a bucket of water unless I showed him. By the third day my shoulders sagged under the weight of the five-gallon buckets as I raced to get the kitchen set up and dinner finished. I'd put Todd in the far corner of the kitchen, setting the buffet counter, just to keep him out from under my feet.

Thunder crackled across the sky. Hail the size of gumballs ham-mered the tarp and bounced across the ground. I stepped next to the cookstove trying to dry off. As I did, water squished inside my boots. My feet had been soaked since the morning of the second day when the rain drenched my jeans, wicked down my socks, and filled my boots. Every morning I'd tried to pour water out of my boots, but the Thinsulate lining captured it like a sponge. I wiggled my toes and the water sloshed. *They're waterproof boots all right. Once the water gets in, it can't get back out.*

Ham steaks sizzled on the griddle. I nudged the spatula under them one by one and flipped them. Out of the corner of my eye I saw Diane, one of the guests, glance at Todd poking along as he set silverware on the buffet table. My toes itched so I curled them inside my boots. *She knows he's a pain to have in the kitchen.* Diane tucked a strand of dark hair behind her ear and shouted over, "Need any help with dinner?"

I shook my head and faked a smile, just like I had at every meal and offer. "Naw. Todd and I have got it. Thanks." I stirred the pota-toes and thought, *Really, I'd love your help, but you're on vacation.*

After dinner I poured steaming hot water into the dishpans. Ruth, another guest, wandered over. "I'd be happy to chip in," she offered. But I turned her away thinking, *You're probably asking because you feel obligated. If I were on vacation, I wouldn't want to do dishes.* I zipped through the stack of dishes while Todd slowly dried each drop on every cup. Grabbing a towel, I whipped it over the rest of the dishes, put them away, and latched the wooden kitchen box.

The rain came down in torrents as twilight fell. The guests and crew sat around the kitchen tables telling stories until the cold evening breeze chased us to our tents. I wandered to my wickiup and ducked under the tarp. I stretched out next to my sleeping bag. *It's going to feel so good to get these wet boots off.*

I lay on my back and drew my knee to my chest. Unlacing my boot, I pulled it off. I quickly pinched my nostrils as I gasped. Whew! My boot stunk! A pungent, sour odor radiated from my foot. Quickly I unlaced the second boot and pulled. Peeling off the socks, I tossed the boots and socks to the bottom edge of the wickiup, so I wouldn't have to smell them all night. My feet looked like prunes and *stunk.* Quickly I tucked them into the red sleeping bag and scooted to the bottom. Flipping on my flashlight, I set my alarm and rolled over to read before I went to sleep.

I cracked my Bible, and it opened to John 13, the story of Jesus wanting to wash Peter's feet. I cackled. It was the first time I could relate to Peter's "No way!" response. His feet were probably dirty and stinky from their day's travel too. Holding my Bible to my chest, I laughed out loud. *There's no way I would want Jesus anywhere near my feet right now. I don't even want to be by my feet. Yuck!*

The rain drummed on my wickiup and splattered against the ground. Chuckling, I reread the passage and saw something else. Peter didn't refuse just because of his dirty feet. He also refused to let Jesus serve him. Jesus *wanted* to serve Peter. *It blessed Jesus when Peter received.* I drew in a deep breath while my mind replayed the week. The guests had wanted to help, but I had refused. I had stolen their blessing by not allowing them to give.

The next morning after we'd stuffed ourselves on French toast, sausage, and eggs, we sat around the kitchen tables talking about the game plan for the day. I downed the last swig of my steaming coffee, stood up, and stacked dirty dishes on my arm. As I turned toward the kitchen, Ruth and Diane helped collect dishes. When I poured the steaming hot water into the dish pans, they both chimed, "You wouldn't mind if we helped, would you?"

"I'd love some help!" At first I felt uncomfortable, but as time wore on, I discovered that by letting the guests help out a little bit, they felt like part of our team and enjoyed their trip a lot more.

*Lord, help me to graciously receive helping hands from others so they too will feel blessed. Amen.*

# 12

# Montana Gang War

*A fool gives full vent to his anger,*
*but a wise man keeps himself under control.*

PROVERBS 29:11

The cool, morning breeze fluttered a strand of long, blond hair in my face. I reached up and tucked it behind my ear. The trail in front of me was dry and dusty, scorched from days in the August sun. It stretched across a flat bench and through a corridor of pines. Amarillo, my copper-colored saddle horse, steadily picked his way down the trail. My body swayed to the rhythm of his steps. Seven loaded pack mules trudged single file behind me. Sighing, I gazed at the peaks that rimmed the canyon as I melted into the saddle. *I am so glad to leave him behind.* This morning I'd almost lost my temper with one of the guys on crew.

Reaching down, I stroked Amarillo's velveteen neck. "Have you ever met anybody as irritating as him?" I shook my head as my mind replayed the events. Yesterday the boss had Matt haul hay to the end-of-the-road camp and asked him to mantie it so it'd be ready for me to load on the mules. But when I drove the gold pickup through the gate this morning, the hay was just stacked under a tarp. I groaned. It'd take at least an hour to get the hay ready to load onto the pack animals. I had a long day ahead of me. After I loaded the mules, I would lead them the 14 miles into Monture base camp, unload and stack the hay, and then have to cook dinner for the crew that was working there.

When I'd asked Matt why he hadn't mantied the hay, he shrugged his shoulders and, with a humorous glint in his eye, asked, "Was I supposed to?" My temper smoldered while I spread out the square canvas mantie tarps on the ground, lugged the hay bales to them, and tied them up. But something scratched down inside me, urging me to ignore him.

My saddle creaked as I shifted my weight and turned around. Glancing at each mule, I checked to make sure the packsaddles rode centered and the loads rocked evenly. Titus, a stocky red mule toward the back of the string, locked eyes with me as he walked up beside the mule in front of him. He grabbed the tarp in his teeth and pulled it so a corner of the hay bale showed. He let go and chomped down on the hay, pulling a chunk loose. The mule squealed and kicked at him. Titus hauled back to escape the flying hoof, breaking the breakaway rope that tied him to that mule. He immediately dropped his nose to chow down on the grass alongside the trail.

"Titus!" I hollered as I bailed out of my saddle. Quickly I tied Amarillo and the lead mule to a tree and stormed to the back of the string. With each step of my boots, dust puffed from the trail. Titus innocently batted his long, red eyelashes as he gobbled grass and eyed me. I snatched his lead rope and snapped, "You know better than that." I led him to the mule in front of him and tucked the canvas in place, covering the hay. After tying Titus to the string, I leveled my eyes with his and commanded, "Now behave!"

Irritated, I walked back to my horse, mounted, nudged Amarillo into a swinging walk, and brooded. *It was as if Titus waited until I was looking to do that.* I pulled a piece of jerky out of my saddlebags and gnawed on it. *No, quit imagining things. I'm just upset from this morning.*

The sun sweltered directly above me. Beads of sweat formed under my hatband. Lifting my cowboy hat, I wiped my forehead and glanced at my lead mule. Her pack pad had moved a couple inches back since we'd left the trailhead. Now it was positioned where it needed to be. My mind whirled back to this morning's fiasco. *I can't believe Matt saddled the mules wrong—again!* Every single one had been saddled wrong even though I'd coached the guy on where to place the pack pads. I'd explained the pads always worked back once the mules strung out on the trail and the loads rocked, so the pads needed to be placed a little higher on the withers.

When I discovered his error and pointed it out, his eyes had laughed at me, although he acted sorry. I wanted to blow my stack, but once again something inside urged me to keep my tongue in check. His antics cost me hours because I'd had to strip off all the saddles. I'd love to tell the boss, but I knew Matt would act innocent and I'd look like the shmuck. *What can I do? I want it resolved now!*

A horsefly buzzed around my head and landed on Amarillo's neck. I squashed it and then pushed my feet into my stirrups and half stood as I turned to check on the mules. Miniature clouds of dust rose with each of the mules' steps. Titus's long ears swiveled forward. Nonchalantly he walked too close to a tree and smacked his load against it. The blow caused the load to tip off kilter. I grimaced. Titus was a round-backed mule and didn't have high enough withers to hold the saddle firmly. *If it tips any more, it's going to roll.* Titus planted all four feet and stopped. The breakaway rope popped and Titus, discovering he was free, walked to a clump of grass and grazed. Irritated with his antics, the mule behind him flattened his ears and bit Titus on the rump. Titus squealed and trotted forward. His pack rocked heavily to the left. *Whoosh!* The packs slid under his belly.

"Titus, you did that on purpose. And the other mules know it too!" I launched out of my saddle and stomped to the back of the string— again. For the next ten minutes I stripped the packs and saddle off Titus while scolding him. "I know you've worked hard this past month, but I haven't had any days off either." Slipping the pack pad in place, I carried on. "You need a spanking!" And I wanted to give him one too, but

I held back. Sweat ran down my back as I reloaded him. I tied him to the mule in front again and left with the words, "No more nonsense, mister. You could get hurt goofing around like that—or cause one of the other mules to get hurt." Tossing my leg over the saddle I groaned. *First Matt and now Titus. I'd like to scream at both of them, but it wouldn't change a thing. What can I do?*

Ahead the trail narrowed to three feet and seemed to barely cling to the side of the mountain. I glanced back to check the mules' loads in case I needed to adjust them before we crossed the cliff. All rode centered. I settled into my saddle and gathered the reins as Amarillo climbed the short hill and rounded the bend. A steep, grassy slope rose straight up from the trail on my right side. On my left, the slant steeply fell into a 50-foot-deep ravine. Amarillo picked his way around the rocks. The mules's hooves drummed on the hard, packed trail.

Suddenly a mule squealed. Snapping my head around, I saw Titus bobbing his head and goofing off. With a glint in his eye, he stared at me, laughing, as if saying, "Watch this!" He skipped forward and banged the front edge of his pack against the cliff. His packs tipped to the left—the drop-off side of the trail.

I gasped and watched in horror as the next few seconds played out in slow motion. The packsaddle on Titus swung with such momentum that it threw him off balance. He stepped sideways to catch himself—right off the trail and into thin air.

Titus's lead rope jerked the mule in front of him off balance, and the one behind him too. In a split-second all seven mules spilled off the trail like dominos and tumbled down the slope. The ground rumbled as each one flipped in somersaults, head over rear. Their loads slammed the hillside and then their hooves hit the ground. Rocks dislodged and slid down. Some of the packs flew off and rolled to the bottom. Then all was still except for the groans of the mules.

In spite of the heat, cold sweat drenched me. My hands shook as I looped the reins around the saddle horn and stepped out of the saddle. My heart pounded in my ears. Crouching on my boots and leaning backward, I skidded down the mountain. Rocks boiled around my feet and washed to the bottom. The mules lay in a pile. The ones who'd lost their loads groaned as they lurched to their feet and shook. Then they plucked at strands of grass. *They look okay.* The others struggled to get to their feet, but their lopsided packsaddles pulled them off-balance so they couldn't stand. Glancing around, I breathed a sigh of relief. *All alive and no broken legs.*

First I stripped loads off all the downed mules, removed the packsaddles, and got the animals to their feet. They were a motley crew with blotches of bald spots from where the rocks had scraped the hair out of their hides. I tromped over to Titus. He was quivering. I snatched his lead rope and hissed, "Do you see what you did to your friends?" I wanted to beat him within an inch of his life. He'd slipped his packs on purpose, and his actions could have killed all the mules. But something inside doused my anger. I'd never beaten an animal, and I wasn't going to start now. Instead I sputtered, "A beating would be too good for the likes of you." I looked him over and was disappointed that he didn't have any swelling from bruises. He wasn't missing a single hair. *What kind of justice is this?*

For the next couple hours I resaddled the mules and led them up to the trail. After lugging the packs up the slope, I loaded them onto the mules and we headed into camp. By the time I crawled into my sleeping bag, I was done in. I didn't roll over all night, but between dreams I faintly remember hearing thumping and squealing from the direction of the corral.

Shafts of dawn light played on the pine boughs when I strolled to the corral. The mules brayed when they saw me, asking for breakfast. I frowned and cocked my head sideways. Titus stood on one side of the corral all by himself. Ducking into the hay shed, I cut strings on a few bales and tossed flakes into the wooden feeders that lined the fence. All the horses and mules bellied up to the mangers—all except Titus.

The wooden corral gate moaned as I slipped through. Curiously, I walked toward Titus. He turned his head. I winced. His left eye was swollen closed, and above it was a knot the size of my fist. Patches of hair were missing all over his body, and in those bald spots were scrapes left from teeth. Several places were swollen and looked distinctively like hoof prints. I chuckled. I'd never seen anything like it and haven't since. There'd been a Montana gang war in the corral last night. The mules had let Titus know what they thought about his antics that had almost gotten them killed. Titus stiffly shuffled over to me. I gently ran my hand over the knot above his eye. "Well, mister, I guess the votes are in. Your popularity ratings went down the tubes, and you got served some Montana justice." I checked him from ears to tail. Nothing was broken other than his rotten attitude.

With my finger I traced a lump on his neck. *Montana justice.* My mind drifted through yesterday's memories. My anger had flared when Titus had tormented me, and I'd wanted him to stop it immediately. There wasn't anything I could do other than restrain my temper, but that was enough. With time everything had worked out. *Maybe the same will be true with Matt.*

Over the next few weeks Matt wore his guise of innocence while he tormented me. Then the boss found a note on the kitchen table saying Matt had quit. His duffel bag was gone—and so were a lot of our possessions. But there was one thing he did leave behind—a key to happy living. When I've done everything I can to change a bad situation and it's still not resolved, it's time to hold back my temper and let God work things out. He always does—in His time. He even made Titus one of the best pack mules in the string! That mule never slipped his loads on purpose again.

> *I'm so glad, Lord, that You're working behind the scenes. Help me be patient and give You opportunities to solve the challenges in my life. Amen.*

13

# Homing Device

*Jesus replied: If anyone loves me, they will
obey me. Then my Father will love them, and
we will come to them and live in them.*

JOHN 14:23 CEV

Lying on my side on the rocky shore, I tossed a pebble into the small mountain lake that was cupped between rocky peaks. It splashed down, the ripples reflecting the colors of the sunset—reds and peaches swirled with white from the clouds. In spite of the beauty that surrounded me, I felt hollow. Today was Sunday, and I'd spent the day clearing trails behind the hunting camp with the boss and a guy on crew. We'd finished late, and at the last minute Larry decided we'd clear the trail up to the lake.

After firing up the chainsaw and zipping through a few downed logs, we arrived and tied the horses near the water. We pulled the sack lunches out of our saddlebags and ate a bite of dinner. I picked up a flat rock and sailed it onto the water, hoping it would skip, but it caught an edge and flipped. Kerplunk. It sank. I sighed. I'd been in the hills every Sunday since I'd started this job months ago. I was a long way from a church. Worse than that, I felt distant from God. *The next time I'll be in town on a Sunday will be in December when this job is over.*

I picked up a round, gray pebble as Larry walked over to his bay gelding and hollered, "Let's head back to camp." D.J., who was sitting alongside the lake, pulled on his tan cowboy hat and meandered to his horse. I stood up, brushed off, and looked to the sunset. The last rays of the sun traced the faint line of the game trail we'd follow. It clung to the side of the steep, grassy mountain and then tumbled down a bank and petered out.

We swung into our saddles, and Larry led us out of the little valley, followed by me on a palomino mare named Sunrise, and then D.J. on his horse. D.J. was leading the pack mule that carried the chainsaw and supplies. The horses and mule picked their way over rocks and around boulders just as the sun slipped behind the mountains and the whole world faded to black.

A cool breeze rolled down the slope. I shivered and untied my wool jacket from behind my saddle. Wiggling it on, I had a sobering thought. I'd ridden many dark nights along trails the horses knew by heart. I didn't care for that, especially when a hoof dislodged a stone and it clattered down a cliff. I always cringed. But tonight was different. Before today, the horses hadn't ever been up here. And we'd bushwhacked cross-country over downed logs, through meadows, through a bog, and alongside hills. And tonight there wasn't going to be any moonlight. *Can the horses find their way back to camp?*

I swayed with the rhythm of Sunrise's steps. I reached down, patted her warm neck, and whispered, "Do you know where you're going?" My heart thudded. Squinting, I tried to see something, but only a lone star twinkled in the sky. I held my hand in front me. Nothing. I waved it. A whisper of air brushed my cheeks. I wanted to pray for direction and safety, but I felt like God was way up in the heavens, beyond that lone star, too far away to reach.

The black night disoriented me. Sunrise trudged up and down the shallow swales along the mountain. I felt like I was riding a roller coaster in slow motion. She pulled at the reins as she dipped her nose. Rocks clattered down the mountain. Sunrise stepped over the edge of a bank. My body tipped back. I gasped and grabbed my saddle horn as Sunrise shinnied down a ways. I knew D.J.'s horse and mule were above me because I could hear rocks being knocked loose. Pebbles grated together under Sunrise's feet. She slid to the bottom. Without pausing, she turned left, her hooves whispering through long grass. *Left?* I gathered the reins and scolded, "Camp is down the canyon to the right!"

From in front of me Larry's voice drifted through the chilly air. "Let her come. Just wrap your reins around the saddle horn."

*Wrap my reins around the saddle horn? You're crazy!* But I did loosen my reins. Sunrise's feet swished through a grassy meadow as we climbed up a gentle hill. Stopping, she lifted her front right foot. I heard it scrape the top of a log that sounded a bit hollow. *Could this be the downed log we crossed this morning when we cut trail in the upper meadow?* She stretched her legs over the obstacle and steadily curved to the right. On my left I could hear the breeze rustling pine boughs, but on my right it whispered through grass. *It is the meadow.*

An owl hooted, the sound fading down the canyon. Each step brought us closer to a different sound. I tipped my head sideways and strained to hear. *What is it? Ah, it's the breeze fluttering the leaves on the cottonwoods that line the creek.* I rubbed my jaw in awe. The horses had just completed a semicircle, walking track for track where we'd guided them this morning.

In a few more steps I could hear water chuckling. The horses' hooves clattered and splashed through the rocky streambed. I put my arm in front of my face, remembering the willow branches that draped the edge of the creek. They brushed past. I leaned forward as Sunrise scrambled up the bank. I knew we were on a game trail that skirted the hillside. *How can they do that? Track for track in the pitch-black night?*

Although more stars twinkled in the sky, I still couldn't see my hand in front of my face. A coyote howled across the canyon, his high-pitched yip rolling over the hills. Far away, another answered. I rubbed my hands together to warm them and then reached into my jacket pockets for my gloves. Pulling them on, I felt Sunrise pick up the pace as her feet swished through long grass again. *Next is the bog, and she'll skirt it the best she can on the right side.* I held my arm in front of my face to block the alder brush as I felt Sunrise sink a bit in the mud and soggy grass. Her shoulders jerked. The mud slurped as she waddled through. The alder branches slapped my right side. Sunrise heaved up a bank and stretched out into a mile-eating walk across another meadow.

I shook my head. Even through the bog the horses continued steadily. How can they do that? Follow the same exact steps except in reverse? It's like God programmed them with a homing device. From my spirit I heard a still small voice: *I've programmed one in you too.* I inhaled and chewed on my lip. I'd gotten so bogged down in my feelings that I'd totally ignored the truth of God's Word. I glanced up at the twinkling stars. *God, You're not far away, beyond the stars. When I was born again in Jesus, You came to live in my heart. Going to church is a great thing, but it is my responsibility to commune with You daily, and that's what I've let slide.*

That's why I felt distanced from Him. The rest of the ride into camp I marveled at the homing device God had installed in horses, and in my mind I spoke with Him about it. Once I started talking with Him, the distance evaporated—I'd found my way home.

*Lord, thank You for always being here for me. Amen.*

14

# Tag's Tail

*My dear brothers and sisters:*
*You must all be quick to listen, slow*
*to speak, and slow to get angry.*

JAMES 1:19 NLT

Birds chirped their morning greetings. The sun rose behind the mountains, crowning them with a golden glow of rays. Our green nylon tents were set up in the Danaher Valley, an enormous grassy meadow framed by steep peaks. I was cooking on a seven-day summer pack trip. Only the crew was awake, packing up gear and catching the stock while the guests slept soundly in their tents.

A cool breeze gently rustled the blue kitchen tarp. I reached for the coffeepot that simmered on the wood cookstove and poured a cup for D.J., the wrangler who sat on a campstool next to the stove. Setting the pot down, I said, "Looks like you've got all the stock caught except Tag—again." Turning toward the kitchen boxes that served as my food preparation counter, I laid out slices of bread to make sandwiches for the crew and guests.

D.J. rubbed his stubbly red beard. "He's being a bugger. Every time…"

I interrupted. "Did you coil up the lead rope and hang the halter from your shoulder so he couldn't see it? When I gentled him that's what I did." I slathered peanut butter on each slice.

D.J. lifted his coffee cup. "I…"

"Did you try slipping the rope over his neck to catch him before you haltered him?"

"He…"

I spooned globs of jam on bread. "Or maybe try haltering him without tossing the rope over his neck. You might need to experiment to see what works the best."

D.J. waved his coffee cup. "But he lets me get to his tail, and then he…"

"He's so easygoing. He can't be that hard to catch." I slipped the sandwiches into plastic bags. "Oh, I'll go get him myself." I untied my apron and stuffed it into the kitchen box. After grabbing a leather halter, I scanned the meadow for Tag. The tall, rawboned, gangly black mule with a tan patch over his left eye stood 100 yards away with his head buried in the tall grass eating. I coiled the lead rope and hung it with the halter over my shoulder. I tucked it close to my body so he wouldn't see it. I ambled into the meadow, and Tag's head came up.

I stopped and bent over, pretending to tie my bootlace so Tag wouldn't think I was trying to catch him.

The mule relaxed. He dropped his head and plucked stems of grass.

I dawdled at an angle to Tag, closing on 50 feet…30 feet…20 feet… 15 feet. With each step, the dew on the grass soaked into my jeans, and cold drops ran down my legs. I shivered. *D.J., this isn't that hard. You could have snuck up on him just like this. I hope you're watching.*

Tag's long, black ears swiveled like periscopes, and one centered on me. While nibbling, he nonchalantly stepped away from me, gaining 15 feet.

My jeans were soaked and clung to my legs. *You cagey little bugger. Let's see if you figure this one out.* I turned around so my back faced him. I stepped backward. Oftentimes when I'd worked with the wild mules, I'd turn around and ease my way next to them. When I had my back facing them they didn't feel as threatened. I think it confused them. Out of the corner of my eye I watched Tag drift a few steps. He turned his tail toward me and continued to chow down.

I took another step backward, and then did it again…and again. *Only seven feet to go…three…*

I rested my left hand on the left side of his rear. I gently gathered the lead rope in my right hand as I baby stepped backward. *Almost to his withers.*

Tag munched away, but as soon as I touched his neck he nonchalantly pivoted away from me, showing me his tail. For the next 15 minutes that mule sauntered off. Just as I got close enough to touch him, he'd do the switcheroo and show me his tail. The worst part was that the guests had filtered over to the kitchen and were lined up in a row watching the circus show. *How humiliating!*

The dew on my jeans had wicked down my socks and dribbled into my boots. I squished with every step. Grabbing the belt loops of my sopping-wet jeans, I wiggled them up. "Tag, do you know how you got your name? Because that tan patch over your left eye looks like a price tag." I clenched my teeth. "Right now I'm thinking of writing some numbers on it!" I stood there steaming and staring at Tag's tail. D.J.'s words drifted through my mind. "But he lets me get to his tail, and then he…"

I now finished the sentence: "Turns his rear and won't let me catch him." *D.J. had tried to tell me, but I kept interrupting him. Why did I assume he didn't know what he was doing? How rude of me. If I would have listened, I wouldn't be standing here soaking wet.*

My eyes glowed green with anger. I growled, "Tag, the gig is up. I'm catching you no matter what."

Tag's ears swiveled. He turned his head sideways, glanced back at me, and batted his long, black eyelashes, as if saying, "Would you like to bet on that?"

Anger surged through me like a bolt of lightning. I reached forward and grabbed that mule's tail with both hands. I planted my boots. He goosed. My knuckles turned white as I held tight. He clamped his tail and swaggered forward.

As if water skiing, I shifted my weight back and dug in my heels. Tag ignored me. He shambled through the meadow.

I bounced and skidded behind that tall, rawboned mule hollering, "Tag, stop it!"

He walked faster and faster.

*He's not going to stop. Now what?* I bumped through the meadow, swinging from side to side, trying to keep my balance as he nearly broke into a trot. Suddenly I had a crazy idea. I yelled at Tag, "I'll teach you!" Then I sat down in the sopping wet grass.

Instantly Tag froze. He swung his head around and looked at me as if to say, "Crazy lady, let go of my tail—you're heavy."

Standing, I hitched up my drenched jeans. Taking the halter off my shoulder I scolded, "If you walk away I'll hang off your tail again." I offered the halter. Quickly he slipped his nose into the loop. I buckled it up.

The guests exploded with laughter. They clapped and whistled.

I walked Tag to the kitchen tarp and handed D.J. the lead rope. "Sorry I interrupted. Now I know what you were trying to tell me."

D.J. chuckled. "Good morning show. What are you going to do for the afternoon?"

*Thank You, Lord, for giving me two ears and one mouth. Please teach me to listen at least twice as much as I talk. Amen.*

# 15

## Hop-a-long

*A cheerful heart is good medicine,*
*but a broken spirit saps a person's strength.*

Proverbs 17:22 nlt

The hot summer breeze whipped Dusty's long, brown tail against my boot and stirrup. The trail skirted the side of a grassy mountain that was dotted with purple asters in bloom. A long line of guests on horseback trudged behind me. As we rounded a bend, a cool, misty breeze swept past. A knot formed in my stomach as I gathered my reins and slowed Dusty, a sturdy gelding. The trail gently sloped down to a narrow creek that gurgled down the mountain. We neared the edge of the water, and I felt Dusty's muscles ripple through his back as he gathered himself on his haunches to jump the creek.

I tapped the reins and sternly said, "Nope! You're not jumping. Remember, one step." Dusty's muscles relaxed and then tensed again. I tapped the reins again to get Dusty to move slowly forward. He stopped and pawed the water with his right front hoof. Cold water splashed my jeans and boots. Then he plunged his foot into the creek and rested his weight on it. I stroked his neck. "Good boy." With a little tension on the reins, I nudged him with my heels. Placing his left front foot in the creek, he relaxed and plodded through the water like a champ. His hooves clattered over the rocks and onto the packed dirt trail. I breathed a sigh of relief and lengthened the reins. "That a boy. You're getting better."

Dusty was the outfit's best guest horse. He wasn't much to look at. He was a solid chocolate-brown with a stocky build and an angular face. His long tail nearly brushed the ground. He loved people, so we could put anyone on him. His character was so true that a bomb could go off next to him, and we figured he'd merely shrug and keep on walking. Until yesterday, that is.

The day before, a 12-year-old named Brian was riding Dusty. When they came to a creek, Dusty decided he wasn't going to get his feet wet. He had crossed hundreds of creeks, but this time instead of calmly walking through the water, he leaped across. I heard a gasp and turned around to see a white-faced Brian hanging on to the saddle horn. Even though I coached Brian on what to do every time we came to a creek, Dusty kept hopping over them.

Today was a layover day. Some of the guests decided to stay in camp and fish by the creek while I led another batch of guests up the trail to a mountain lake. Because Brian had decided to fish, I saddled up Dusty in hopes of working out the creek kink.

My body rocked to the beat of Dusty's stride. Normally I enjoyed visiting with the guests as I rode down the trail. But today I was so focused on Dusty that the guests didn't even exist in my world. I glanced at the narrow ribbon of trail that wound around the steep slope in front of me. Throughout the rest of the trip, we'd ride across hillsides just like this and cross creeks that tumbled down the mountain. My tummy churned. I shuddered as I remembered stories of horses that jumped creeks along narrow trails…but didn't land on the other side. They'd lost their footing and fallen off the trail and down the mountain.

*What am I going to do?* My mind chugged though options. *If Dusty doesn't straighten out today, I could put a more experienced rider on him.*

I shook my head. I couldn't take the chance. I didn't dare put Brian on Czar, my saddle horse, because he was barely trained. I slumped in the saddle. My heart felt heavy. *If things don't work out today, one of the crew will have to ride out and get another guest horse. I hate to pull Dusty out of the dude string. He's been such a great horse, and they're in short supply. God, I need Your help. What should I do?*

Ravens circled overhead, playing on the afternoon breeze. The hooves of the horses drummed down the trail until it widened onto a soggy, grassy bench. I reined Dusty around the bog to the creek crossing. "This is going to be your test, buddy." Although the creek only flowed a couple feet wide, the creek bed was about eight feet across. It cut through the hill in a deep furrow, about two-and-a-half feet straight down. I'd have to let Dusty bunch his feet underneath him so he could ease his front feet over the edge. After he stepped his hind legs down, I'd ask him to walk through the water and scramble up the bank on the other side. The saddle creaked as I centered my weight in case he jumped. Easing the slack out of the reins I whispered, "Remember, no jumping."

Through the saddle I felt Dusty's back muscles tighten as he stepped to the edge. I swallowed. Holding my hands steady, I tapped the reins. "Easy." Dusty hesitated and then bunched his feet underneath him. Gently I nudged him with my heel. "One step," I commanded. He swung his right front foot forward. I leaned back as he dropped his front feet into the creek bed. "That a boy! Now your hind legs." Squeezing my legs, I kept a little tension on the reins. He scooted his back legs over the edge, bunching his feet on the narrow creek bed so he wouldn't get them wet. Dusty teetered for a second while I held my breath. The grass rustled as the guest and horse behind me stepped up to the edge and stopped.

Dusty shifted his weight backward.

I tightened the reins. "No," I reminded him.

His muscles tensed as he pushed off with his hind legs. He hopped into the air—but only flew a couple feet. He stopped suddenly—in midair—almost like he'd come to the end of a rope. He landed with his front feet splashing in the water. The unexpected stop threw my weight forward. I sat upright in the saddle. *What happened?*

Dusty wiggled his rear and chugged backward, scooting his feet out of the creek. He planted himself firmly, essentially digging in his heels.

I gripped him with my legs and said, "One step, Dusty."

But the gelding insisted on jumping. He launched from his hind legs again. In midair he jerked to a stop. When he came down, his front feet slammed the water, spraying me with cold droplets. Quickly he scooted back and wiggled his rear. It was as if his hind feet were tangled in wire.

Frowning, I leaned over and looked underneath his belly at his legs and hooves. Nothing.

One of the guests stifled a laugh. The rest broke out with gales of laughter. I glanced at them. They sat on their horses, laughing and pointing at Dusty's rear. Stretching in the saddle, I turned and looked. When Dusty had stepped down into the furrow, his tail had stayed on the grassy bank. When the horse behind us came up to the edge, it stepped on Dusty's tail and pinned it to the ground. Every time Dusty tried to hop across the creek, he'd launch into the air until he hit the length of his tail. Then he was pulled back as his tail acted like a giant rubber band. A grin cracked across my face and laughter rose from my belly. "Ouch!"

I patted Dusty's neck. "So what do you think about jumping creeks now?"

After the guest and horse stepped aside, I nudged Dusty forward. Gingerly he placed his right front foot into the water. Slowly he eased forward across the creek and scrambled up the bank.

The rest of the ride I fellowshipped with the guests and laughed. And as far as I know, Dusty never tried to jump a small creek again. I've never forgotten how God cured him. I could almost hear God telling me, "Rebecca, don't be so serious. I'm here with you. I'll help. Let's have some fun doing this together."

> *Lord, remind me to quit being so serious that I forget those around me. Your solution to whatever I'm facing is only one hop away. Amen.*

16

# Keeping the Beat

*Do not let this Book of the Law depart from your
mouth; meditate on it day and night, so that
you may be careful to do everything written in
it. Then you will be prosperous and successful.*

JOSHUA 1:8

Bzzzz. Bzzzz. A horsefly bit my leg. "Ouch!" Saddle leather creaked as I shifted to slap the bug. Groggily I shook my head to wake up. I squinted. *How long have I been sleeping?* The brilliant sun beat down. A trickle of sweat rolled between my shoulder blades. I blinked and yawned. Amarillo had his nose buried in a clump of grass. Disgusted because we'd stopped, I looked behind me. Seven mules loaded with packs also cropped grass. *At least their loads are centered and nobody's tangled up.*

I lightly swatted Amarillo's neck. "You weren't supposed to stop when I napped." I turned in the saddle and hollered, "Heads up!" The mules raised their heads and stared at me. I nudged Amarillo forward, gradually gaining speed into a mile-eating walk. Horse and mule hooves kicked up dust from the trail. In a couple miles I gritted my teeth to stifle a yawn. My eyes watered, my throat tightened, my ears popped. In a few steps I yawned again and almost nodded off. Shaking my head to wake up, I wondered, *How am I going to stay awake?*

73

Time was my enemy. It was late August and the last big push to pack hay into camp before hunting season. The summer season had been busy with pack trips, and it seemed like I hadn't had a chance to catch my breath before the hay runs began. These weeks were some of the most grueling of the season. Every day we worked from "can see" to "can't see."

Every minute was work. At dawn's first light we slung mantied hay bales, some weighing 110 pounds, onto the mules' packsaddles. After riding 14 miles into base camp and unloading, we rode back to the end-of-the-road corral. By lantern light we ate dinner and mantied a stack of bales for the next day. Then we crawled into our sleeping bags.

I'd lost so much weight that I was a rack of bones. Not only was I physically tired, but my morning Bible study had become a quick glance at a Scripture verse before I slapped my Bible shut. Each day the gauge of my spiritual tank registered a notch lower. *I know I'm slipping. I can't keep the beat in my life. God, how do I balance my time between work and You when I can't squeeze another drop of time out of the day?*

Miles rolled past as Amarillo plodded the trail. My head bobbed. I slouched in the saddle and napped. One of the mules squealed, and I bolted awake and turned in the saddle. We'd drifted off the trail into a small meadow, and two mules were squabbling over a clump of grass. I barked at them, "Knock it off!" The string of mules was huddled in one bunch. I glared at them and fumed at myself. *Rebecca, you've got to stay awake or you're going to have a wreck.*

The problem was that when I fell asleep, Amarillo would lose the beat. He'd plod slower and slower until he stopped. And so did the mules. When a string stops, it spells trouble. If the animals aren't moving forward single file, they're wandering around and getting tangled up in the trees, the brush, or each other. My string of mules was like having seven 1100-pound bombs tied together on one rope. If one torches off, all of them might blow. I'd lived through enough mule wrecks in my life; I didn't want to add another notch to my belt.

My saddle creaked as I turned to watch the mules. I hollered, "Heads up!" Amarillo snatched his last bite and slowly stepped forward. The long line of mules unwound, and I nudged Amarillo up to speed.

A hawk lazily drifted overhead, occasionally screeching. The sun lulled me and I yawned. *Stay awake, Rebecca!* I bit my lip until my eyes watered. My body rocked in the saddle as we snaked through a long corridor of lodgepole pines. I'd ridden this trail so many times that I knew every rock and every tree. *How can I keep the beat?*

By the time we rolled into hunting camp, I was ready to prop toothpicks in my eyelids to keep them open. My blood got pumping when I unloaded the mules, and I was wide awake by the time I pulled out of camp and headed down the trail. But before a mile passed under Amarillo's hooves, my chin bumped my chest. My snoring woke me up. The next eight miles I slapped my face, pinched my cheeks, and did everything I could think of to stay awake. *How am I going to stay awake tomorrow?*

That night when the guys and I mantied hay, we were short four bales. I volunteered to drive the pickup to the pasture to grab them. The sun slipped in back of a mountain as I slid behind the wheel. Flicking on the lights, I relaxed in the cushy seat and my eyes drooped. A warning bell went off in my head. *Stay awake!* Glancing at the old radio, I noticed a tape sticking out. I pushed it in and cranked the speakers. Amy Grant! I rocked down the road. By the time I reached the pasture, I'd hatched a plan.

The next morning I woke to a dry breeze rattling through the pine boughs. It was going to be another scorcher. I could barely keep my eyes open as I quickly scanned a verse before packing my Bible away. After I'd strung out the mules on the trail, I grinned and dug into my saddlebags. On a regular trip, with guests around, all electronic devices were outlawed by the boss. I grinned as I pulled out my portable player. *Only Amarillo and the mules are around, and I know they won't be offended.* I jury-rigged my headphones behind my cowboy hat and let Amy blast. Instantly Amarillo picked up his step, and we cruised down the trail.

I rocked in the saddle to the beat as we splashed through the river. One mile passed, then two. But by the time we reached the long stand of pines, my eyelids drooped, I yawned, and my head bobbed. The sun warmed my back as I slumped in the saddle. Miles later I opened my eyes. My body was swaying. Confused, I blinked. Amarillo was still cruising to the beat of Amy Grant, and the mules were trailing right along behind. I reached down and patted Amarillo's neck. "That was supposed to keep me awake!" I laughed. "But it did better than that. Even with my earphones on, you kept the beat. Good boy!"

Over the next few days I caught up on my sleep from the saddle. Not that I intended to, but I couldn't stay awake. The music worked so well in keeping the beat for Amarillo that I decided to put my headphones on at night and listen to Scripture as I fell asleep. God's Word revived my spirit and started a habit I still do today.

I encourage you to meditate on God's Word at night. Doing that helps me keep the spiritual beat all day, and it may help you too.

*Lord, thank You for giving me Your Word to set the pace for my life. Amen.*

# 17

# Night Vision

*I praise you, LORD, for being my guide. Even in
the darkest night, your teachings fill my mind.*

PSALM 16:7 CEV

The moon was merely a sliver in the cobalt-blue sky. An owl hooted, its voice drifting down the canyon on the cool breeze. Although a few stars twinkled, the night was black. I stumbled down the trail to the creek, a five-gallon metal bucket in each hand. I squinted. *How do the guys do this? I can't see a thing.* I took a few more steps and stubbed my toe on a rock. "Ouch!" I flicked on my flashlight that I held in my left hand sandwiched next to the bucket handle. I'd grown up in a small town and never spent much time in the dark. At night the street lights glowed on every corner, and when I was indoors light switches were always handy.

I directed the beam of light down the winding trail, tracing a picture in my mind. I clicked off the flashlight. *I'm going to get this yet.* But after a few more steps I stumbled off the trail and into the brush. I flicked on the light, walked several steps, and clicked it off. Then on again. Then off again. By the time I dipped the buckets into the creek it must have looked like I was sending Morse Code messages.

I felt my way up the trail with water sloshing onto my leather boots. "Why did I tell Richard I'd have dinner waiting for him? If I would have kept my mouth shut, I wouldn't be hauling water in the dark," I growled. My shoulders sagged under the weight of the buckets. I was the cook in hunting camp, and today was the last day of the hunt. Tonight Richard was bringing in the string of mules we'd use to pack out the hunters and gear tomorrow morning. I had a tradition that whenever the guys on crew rode out early in the morning or came in late at night, I'd have a hot meal simmering on the stove for them.

My foot skidded on a pebble. A bucket banged against my leg and splashed water on my jeans. *Would it matter if I skipped cooking this one time?* The cook tent glowed from the propane lanterns. When I brushed aside the tent flap, a blast of heat from the woodstoves swept past me. Water sloshed as I stepped over the base log anchoring the structure. Setting the buckets on the dirt floor by the serving counter, I reached up and shut off the hissing lanterns. The tent plunged into darkness. *Now to check the horses in the corral and then off to bed I go.* "That is—until Richard rides in," I muttered.

I groped my way alongside the long, plank table. Pushing the tent flap aside, I stepped out. It was so dark I couldn't even tell where the trail to the corral was. I fumbled a few steps. Fifty feet away a twig snapped. I froze and held my breath. *The guides and the guests are all in bed.* My heart pounded. *What is that?*

I crouched as I switched on the flashlight, sweeping the beam to and fro through the woods. Two eyes glowed. I swallowed hard. An ear flicked. I closed my eyes. *Just a deer. Maybe part of my problem with the dark is that I watched too many scary movies as a kid. I don't want to be a wimp, but the most frightening parts of ghost stories always happen at night.* My flashlight bore a hole in the blackness as I scoured the woods. I cautiously tiptoed down the trail. At the corral, I was careful to shine the beam in the air over the backs of the horses and mules. They don't care for flashlights, and I didn't want to start a stampede. The animals were contentedly munching hay out of the mangers. I turned toward my tent. *Buck up, Rebecca. Shut off the light.* I flicked off the flashlight and slowly felt my way on the trail using the toes of my boots. My heart thumped the whole time, but I only clicked the light on a couple times. I took off my boots and melted into my sleeping bag. My body ached from splitting wood and hauling water. I rolled over and grouched, "I got up at three o'clock this morning to cook. I'm bushed. Why did I tell Richard I'd have dinner waiting for him?" Within moments I fell asleep.

The whinnying of horses jarred me awake. Drumming hoofbeats drifted through the still night. I sat up and shivered as cool air seeped into my sleeping bag. I stretched, slipped into my jeans, and laced my boots. Shrugging on my jacket, I reached for my flashlight and strolled to the corral.

Camp was abuzz. Several guys stumbled out of their tents to help unload the hay that was packed on the mules. One crew member lit a Coleman gas lantern. It hissed as he hung it in the tree by the tack shed. Richard untied the mules from each other, retying them individually to the hitching rail.

I strolled over to him. "Did you have a good ride?"

He nodded and handed me the lead to a tall, rawboned, black mule. "I put the kitchen stuff you wanted on John. If you'll lead him to the cook tent, I'll be up in a minute to unload."

Grabbing the rope, I turned and led John out of the circle of lantern light and into the darkness. After several steps I walked off the trail and tripped over a short bush. Catching myself, I pulled my flashlight out of my jacket pocket. "John, don't mind the light." I flicked the switch. John snorted and backed away. Quickly I located the trail and flipped the light off. I tugged on the lead rope, but John didn't move. I tugged again. "C'mon, buddy." Apprehensively, he stepped forward.

Within ten feet I had wandered off the trail again and flashed the light. John's nostrils flared, and he shook his head. Switching off the beam, I urged him forward. He planted his feet and didn't budge.

Footsteps approached and Richard said, "Give him a second for his eyes to adjust. The flashlight blinded him."

I relaxed my hand and tipped my head. "The flashlight blinded him?"

Richard stopped next to me. "When you do that, how can you see?"

"Do what?"

In the darkness I heard Richard shift his weight. "Keep flicking on the flashlight."

My mind whirled. *How can I see when I flick on the flashlight?* Confused, I replied, "I can't see without it."

"That's because you haven't trained your eyes. After you shut off the light, it takes a few minutes for your eyes to adjust to the dark—sometimes as long as a half an hour before you can see clearly."

"Oh." I put the flashlight into my pocket. Is that what I was doing wrong? Before my eyes could adjust to the dark, I clicked the flashlight and blinded myself again?

Richard's boots ground on the dirt as he stepped forward. "And don't stare directly at what you want to see. Look above it, to the side, or below it."

Nobody had ever told me that. I stepped forward, following the sounds of his boots. John nudged me with his nose as he trailed behind. I focused my eyes above the trail and felt my way.

"And concentrate on seeing shapes, not details or color." Richard walked another 20 feet and then stopped. "Let's unload here."

I held John's lead rope as Richard untied the loads. The packs flopped onto the ground. Tying the pack ropes on the saddle, he said, "It doesn't happen overnight. It takes time and practice to train your eyes."

"If you take John back to the corral, I'll get your dinner going," I said. After lighting the propane lanterns, I laid chunks of wood on the red-hot coals inside the cookstove. While grilling his steak, I mulled over the idea of training my eyes to see in the dark. Using the flashlight was convenient, but in a big picture way, it defeated my goal.

I slid the coffeepot over the hot spot on the stove and yawned. *I guess I better put on another bucket of water for dishes.* At the thought of doing dishes again, I groaned. *It's going to be another hour before I can crawl into bed.* That thought arrested me. *What am I muttering about?* Richard hadn't asked me to serve him a hot meal. I had offered.

A war had been going on inside of me. In my heart doing something for Richard sounded like a good idea. But in my head I wanted to do what was convenient—go to bed and forget about him. All evening my thoughts had been flicking between my heart and my head. As soon as I flashed the light on me and my needs, it blinded me and I couldn't see Richard's needs. I knew what to do. Follow God's Word by doing to others as I want them to do to me—and do it with a joyful heart, not begrudgingly.

I poured hot water into a wash pan as Richard stepped into the tent. After splashing water on his face and washing his hands, he sat down and dug in. Between mouthfuls, he told me about his ride. After scraping his plate clean, he set down his fork. Dabbing his brown moustache with a napkin, he contentedly leaned back. "Thanks for cooking dinner. That hit the spot."

I nodded. A warm feeling flooded my heart. As I cleaned up, I thought about Richard's advice for walking in the dark. I realized I'd never thought about my heart having eyes or how spiritually blinded I became when I focused on my own comfort. I discovered that when I train my heart to follow God's Word, I can see clearly.

*Lord, open the eyes of my heart so I clearly see where You're guiding me. Amen.*

18

# Hahn Pass

*Hear my prayer, O Lord God Almighty;*
*listen to me, O God of Jacob.*

Psalm 84:8

Golden sunlight danced across the white canvas wall tent, making it glow inside. The fire in the cookstove crackled and popped, sending waves of heat through the tent. Lifting the five-gallon water bucket, I filled the blue enamelware coffeepot that sat on the stove. A splash of water hit the surface. In a cloud of steam, the water danced and sizzled off the edge. *That's exactly what I feel like my prayers are doing—rolling off.* I'd been praying constantly for weeks, but nothing had changed. *Is God hearing me?*

Setting the bucket on the dirt floor, I glanced at the tall stack of wood I'd split and hauled next to the stove. *That'll hold me until tomorrow and my checklist is done. I need a break and some think time. There's no better place to think than from the saddle.* I pulled my tan wool jacket from the nail where it hung by the door. Slipping it on, I hustled to the corral and saddled Amarillo.

Camp robber jays circled overhead and squawked. They landed on the hitching rail, strutting up and down while looking at me and asking for bread. I grinned. "You little beggars will have to wait until tomorrow." I swung my leg over the saddle and lined Amarillo out in

82

a slow trot. The sun glistened off the snowcapped peaks outlining the canyon. Brilliant-gold larch trees contrasted against the deep-green pines and flaming-red huckleberry bushes that dotted the hillsides. Reaching down, I stroked Amarillo's copper-colored neck. "What a beautiful fall day. A great break from weeks of frustration."

The trouble had started when one of the guys on crew up and quit with no warning. One day he was there; the next he packed his duffel bag and drove out the driveway. *What was he thinking?* It was the middle of the hunting season, and we needed every one of us to run the camp. He'd let us all down. Furiously I prayed that God would bring the right person to join crew—someone who would stay the rest of the season. The boss had passed the word to friends and other outfitters. He even ran an ad in the paper and called a job service. Meanwhile, I prayed some more, but it seemed to no avail. Instead, all of us picked up the slack. Now we were worn thin.

My days started at three o'clock, cooking breakfast for the hunters, followed by hauling water and washing dishes. After splitting wood and cutting kindling for the tents, I swept them out. I strolled over to the corral to doctor horses. On the way back to the cook tent, I gathered the Coleman gas lanterns to wash the sooty glass globes and fill them with fuel. By then it was usually time to line out dinner.

Amarillo's metal shoes clicked against the rocks as he trotted down the trail. With my finger I twirled a strand of his mane. "I get tired thinking about it. And I'm not the only one who's been working to the bone." Yesterday Bob had ridden out with elk meat destined for Missoula loaded on the mules. Today he planned to stack two tons of hay and then haul it to the end-of-the-road area, where he would load some of it onto the mules. Right now he was probably riding the trail toward camp. I leaned back in the saddle and grumbled, "God, how do I know if You can hear me?"

The dusty trail wound around the mountain and into a canyon that led to Hahn Pass. Sweat glistened behind Amarillo's ears and dripped down his neck. I slowed him to a walk as we climbed into the pass. The long, winding, grassy meadow was rimmed on both sides by steep mountains littered with boulders and shale rockslides. Several ravens cawed and circled overhead, playing on the wind currents and looking for dinner. I glanced up the steep hillside to the east. I'd always wanted to climb up there and check out the view. I glanced at my watch. *If I don't stay too long, I can do it today.* Excitedly, I dismounted and tied Amarillo to a tree. I started my climb.

I scrambled over boulders and shinnied across patches of shale until I sat on a rocky ledge overlooking the valley. The sun was high in the sky and had warmed the rocks. I lay flat on my back and nestled in. Gazing into the blue sky I watched the billowy white clouds lazily float past. A jet stream etched a white ribbon. The air was still, and the world was quiet. Then I heard something. It sounded like voices. I lifted myself to my elbows and looked at the thread of a trail below me. *Nothing.* But as soon as I lay down, I could hear the boss's voice as clear as if he were standing 10 feet away.

I sat up and scanned the trail. *Nothing.* The voices became louder and clearer, and now I could hear the hunters. *Am I hearing things?* My eyes scanned the meadow in a zigzag pattern. Amarillo looked the size of an ant. Suddenly his head popped up and he whinnied. I gripped the warm rock and hung over the edge, squinting in the direction he was staring. Even though I was the one with the birds-eye view, I still couldn't see signs of people. Finally three little dots rode into sight. *They must be almost half a mile away, and they aren't talking with raised voices. I can hear them as clearly as if they are sitting next to me.* I cocked my head. *I didn't know sound traveled up.*

The next 15 minutes the boss and hunters casually traversed the meadow. They rode over to Amarillo, glanced around, and then rode down the trail toward camp. I sat on that rock baffled. I watched their every move and could hear their every word, but they didn't know I was on the ledge. *How can that be?* In my spirit I heard, *It's the same with Me.* My heart leaped. My words weren't like water bouncing off a hot stove. They traveled up to God. He heard my every whisper.

Peace filled my heart, followed by an understanding that even though I wasn't seeing any results from my prayers, that didn't mean anything. I had to have faith that God was at work behind the scenes.

I watched the guys ride out of sight. I clambered down the mountain and followed them into camp. While dinner simmered on the woodstove, Bob rode in pulling string. We all trooped down to the hitching rail to help him unload. Bob swung his leg over the saddle, stepped down, and pointed at the boss. "You won't believe what happened in Missoula."

Larry tipped his head sideways.

Bob chuckled. "A friend of mine named Jeff just got back into town, and he's hunting for a job."

When we broke camp and headed home, it was like God had everything arranged. Riding into the end-of-the-road area, we saw Jeff waiting patiently. After talking with him, Larry hired him on the spot.

Although Jeff didn't have much experience with packing mules, he threw his heart into the job, pulled his own weight, and stayed until the end of the season. He turned out to be a perfect fit in our crew. Whenever I wonder if God hears my prayers, I remember that afternoon on the ledge. I'm firmly convinced my prayers *always* travel all the way up to heaven.

> *Lord, thank You for showing me that although I don't always see results to my prayers, You are always watching, listening, and working behind the scenes. Amen.*

# 19

# Black Ice

*When they call on me, I will answer; I will be with them in trouble. I will rescue them and honor them.*

PSALM 91:15 NLT

Standing next to the red, gooseneck trailer, I held the lead rope of a copper-colored gelding and pulled up the collar on my winter jacket. Thick, black clouds roiled over the snowy peaks that rimmed the valley. I patted Amarillo. "Remember, you've got to push to get in." Steam from my breath rolled through the still air. Eleven horses and mules stood crosswise in the trailer. By loading the trailer tight, the horses and mules could lean against each other for support and they traveled better. The trailer floor groaned and shook as Amarillo shouldered himself against the horse in front of him. Quickly I closed and latched the door.

Turning, I scanned the pasture for my black German shepherd named Rye. I whistled through my fingers. She looked up from her mouse-hunting adventure and came running full bore. I reached down to pet her. "Good girl." I frowned as an icy wind thundered down the rocky canyon and buffeted me. When I'd left home earlier today, it was sunny and the weather forecast hadn't predicted any changes. Rye leaned against my leg, and I scratched behind her ear.

"We better make some tracks. I don't want to get caught hauling this load in that storm. It looks nasty."

I pulled open the cab door on the yellow, two-ton truck. Rye bounded onto the bench seat. I slid in, cranked the engine, and eased down the gravel road. The boss had just bought this heavy-duty truck with dual rear wheels to haul the heavily loaded horse trailer. The truck and trailer were as long as a semitrailer.

It was November, and we were out of the backcountry for two days between hunts. Because the snow was piling up, I was shuttling the horses and mules to a pasture that hadn't been grazed this year. That way nobody would have to toss them hay while we were in the hills. Even if there was a blizzard, the horses and mules would be able to paw through and eat lush grass.

A flurry of snowflakes whirled around the truck as I pulled out onto the highway. I clicked the windshield wipers on and petted Rye. "This might get ugly," I said. The big, wet flakes stuck to the windshield between swipes. Rye sat at attention, ducking and trying to see out. I flicked the wipers on high and leaned forward. Fog crept up the inside of the windows. Turning the defroster on high, I reached into my back pocket, pulled out my red bandana, and wiped the windshield.

Thick flakes dumped from the sky, covering the blacktop and turning everything white. My world drifted in so I could only see a couple car-lengths in front of me. The truck groaned as I shifted down. The rear tires slipped sideways a few inches. The tires grabbed, and the truck jerked forward, causing the horses and mules to slam against the side of the trailer, which caused the truck to slip again. The trailer fishtailed as the horses and mules slammed against the side again. My heart skipped a beat. Pulling my foot off the accelerator, I let the truck slow to 20 miles per hour, then 15. Scooting to the edge of the seat, I squinted, trying to see the white line on the edge of the road.

My hands tightened on the steering wheel as I reviewed the stretch of road ahead of me. The highway ran through a narrow canyon where it wrapped itself around a mountain. A sheer rock face rose out of the left side of the pavement, the right side dropped down a 100-foot cliff into a river. There wasn't even a guard rail on that stretch. I shuddered as I remembered watching two semis pass each other… without any room to spare. *And that was on dry roads.*

The defroster blasted warm air in my face. My eyes felt dry. I blinked. *How about I park the truck right here in the middle of the highway…at least until I can see a white line or something?* But I'd heard stories of folks getting killed by cars ramming into them because of low visibility. *I have to keep going—for now.* My mind shuffled through possibilities. *Is there any place to pull off?* I chewed on my lip, tracing the highway in my mind. *Nothing short of home where I can park this long beast.*

I wiped my sweaty palm on my jeans as we inched past a green mile marker. "Hang on, Rye. The cliff's next." Rye scooted her rear end underneath her and leaned forward. As we entered the opening of the canyon, the wind howled and slammed the truck. My heart pounded in my ears as I tightened my icy grip on the steering wheel. The engine bogged down as we slowly climbed uphill. The horses and mules restlessly shifted their weight, causing the trailer to gently sway. I held my breath, not wanting to move. Squinting, I could see the ruffled pattern in the snow where the edge of the pavement stopped and the narrow gravel shoulder began.

Up, up, up we inched around the mountain and into the curve. The snow fell so thickly that I couldn't see the sheer rock face on my left or the raging river on my right. The weight of the truck tipped toward the river because that was the direction the pavement sloped through the curve. Everything was blindingly white. It was like driving by feel. Suddenly the engine raced. The rear tires spun. They couldn't get traction to pull uphill. *Black ice!* I pulled my foot off the gas pedal to let the tires grab. The weight of the trailer slammed the hitch on the truck, swinging the rear end of the truck toward the river.

The whole road was coated with black ice. I grabbed the steering wheel in terror as the minutes unfolded in slow motion. The truck continued to slide uphill, but the slope of the pavement toward the river was so steep that the rear of the truck twisted downhill. I could hear the tires crackling across the ice. Gravity pulled us toward the river. The momentum, built up from the weight of 12 horses and mules, pushed on the hitch and caused the truck and trailer to jackknife.

Cold sweat beaded on me as the truck skidded 90 degrees sideways. My back was toward the river. The tires grated against the gravel on the shoulder. *Oh no! We're going over!* Trying to look out the window behind me, I pushed my feet into the floor and stretched. The tires were nearly over the edge. I knew there was no way the truck could correct. *If I go over the cliff, I'm dead. I've got to jump out before the truck tumbles into the river!*

I clenched my teeth, grabbed Rye by the scruff of her neck, and reached for the door handle. The engine of the truck roared and the wind whipped as I cracked the door open—and stared into the side of the trailer. The trailer had buckled so far that it was nearly bumping my door. It was skidding 90 degrees sideways on the highway too. We were taking up both lanes. There wasn't any way I could jump out without getting run over by the trailer. I was trapped in a tomb!

I pulled the door closed, let go of the steering wheel, and screamed, "Jesus!"

The tires skidded on the gravel and the engine roared. I closed my eyes and let my head flop against the window behind me. "Lord, You've got to straighten this out!"

As soon as I screamed His name, it was as though He wrapped me inside a cocoon far removed from the chaos. I'd never experienced anything like it. It was almost as if I had been snatched out of that moment in time. Even the sounds became dull. I felt protected and safe.

Although the truck and trailer still skidded uphill and around the curve, tires scraping along the shoulder, it was as if an unseen force grabbed hold of the rig and pulled it back into its own lane—against gravity. As it did, the trailer fell into place behind it. By the time we'd topped the hill and slid down the other side, the feeling of being in the cocoon faded. I shook uncontrollably. My mouth was dry and sweat dripped down my back.

The rest of the way home was on black ice. I didn't dare stop. With white knuckles I gripped the steering wheel until I inched into the ranch yard. Shutting off the engine, I leaned my head on the steering wheel. I was exhausted. Tears dripped down my face. Never had I been that close to death and witnessed God's delivering power.

Rye nuzzled me with her wet nose and whined. I lifted my head, and she licked a tear off my cheek. Scratching her ear I said, "Okay, girl. Let's get these critters unloaded. They don't know how blessed they are."

*Lord, now I know that You still rescue people today. Amen.*

# 20

## Sirocco

*We can rejoice, too, when we run into problems
and trials, for we know that they are good for
us—they help us learn to endure. And endurance
develops strength of character in us, and character
strengthens our confident expectation of salvation.*

ROMANS 5:3-4 NLT

Waves of heat rolled off the large stove as the fire crackled and popped. Sitting on the wood bin next to it, I pulled on my winter boots. Grabbing my mittens and jacket off the nail by the door, I slipped outside into the winter wonderland. A chickadee's whistle floated on the frosty, still air. Although it was already the beginning of April, the winter snow that had drifted to the top of the eaves still lay in soggy piles throughout the ranch yard. I pulled on my mittens and zipped up my jacket. My boots crunched through the icy crust as I headed to the barn to feed the mares, one of which was pregnant.

I glanced at the hills that glowed from the golden sunrise. I felt rested and relaxed for the first time since the outfitting season ended. Although I loved riding my horse in the mountains 24/7, it was tough. I'd jumped in with both feet and struggled to learn everything I could about working in the wilderness. By the time December rolled around, I was physically, emotionally, and spiritually exhausted.

It had taken me until spring to recuperate. I sighed. Next month the outfit would shift into full gear again. *Am I ready for another season? God, could You make it easier this year?*

The smell of alfalfa greeted me as I stepped into the barn. With my pocketknife, I cut the strings on a bale and carried a flake to a stall. The metal wheels on the door squealed as I rolled it aside. Snipe, a bay mare with a long, wiggly, white stripe down her face, nickered. Warm air from her body heat rushed past me, carrying the pungent and sour smell of afterbirth. Snipe nickered and nodded her head at me before turning to the colt that lay curled up on the straw. He was still wet from amniotic fluid.

My heart skipped a beat. "Oh, Snipe, what a beautiful baby!" Tossing the hay into the feeder, I sat on the edge of a wooden bunk and took inventory of the colt. He was bay, like his mother, with four heavy-boned legs and a small white star on his forehead. Resting my elbows on my knees, I cradled my chin in my hands. "The name Sirocco fits you."

Snipe snuffled and nudged her colt's bony rear, encouraging him to stand. The baby awkwardly flipped one front leg in front of him. While bringing his other front leg forward, he propped himself and scooted a couple feet across the dirt floor before tumbling into a heap. I muffled a giggle with my mitten.

The mama licked her son's hind legs. The colt shook his head. The stubble of his curly black mane rippled. He lay on his chest with one leg in front of him, the other tucked under. He rocked forward and back, straining. He gathered his hind legs underneath him and pushed. His rear popped up with so much momentum that he launched forward, plowing his nose through the dirt as he fell face first. I grimaced. "Ouch!" I chewed on my lip while watching him struggle. On the next attempt, he crossed his front legs and pushed, tumbling to the side. He stopped and lay on his chest, panting. Wisps of steam escaped his flared nostrils. It was almost as if he was figuring out how to use his new stilt-like legs.

Sirocco twitched his fuzzy, teardrop, shaped ears and shook his head. Pushing the stilts in front of him, he drew himself up. Bracing his front legs at angles with each other, he made a hopping motion with his hind legs. His front hooves skidded sideways. In slow motion he sank to the floor, doing the splits. I clenched my fists. "Argh. How painful!" I stepped toward him to help straighten his legs. They looked as if they might pop out of his shoulder sockets, but deep in my spirit I heard, *Leave him be. He needs to struggle to get strong…just like you.*

*Like me?* I'd never thought of my struggles making me strong. My mind whirled as it flashed back. I thought of getting kicked, bit, and trampled into the mud when I took the job of gentling 19 wild mules and a horse. I'd learned to be single-minded and persistent. When my dog Kai died, I'd learned to quit wallowing in regret and to forgive myself. Through Tag the mule and his elusive behavior I'd learned to listen to others. Jackknifing on the black ice showed me that God still delivers folks today. The list was endless.

The colt licked his lips and made a sucking noise. I leaned back against the hay feeder. *Poor thing's hungry.* Snipe nuzzled the colt's face. She licked his star. The colt closed his eyes as he enjoyed the warm tongue brushing his forehead. Snipe stepped to the side and nickered. The colt opened his eyes, propped his front legs in front of him, and gathered his hind legs under his belly. He lurched up on all fours. His body wobbled to the left. Overcompensating, he leaned to the right. He scrambled to keep his legs underneath him. Sidestepping like a tap dancer he scooted across the floor. His legs tangled up. *Whop!* He flopped onto his right side.

I grabbed the plank on the wooden hay feeder that I was leaning against. I wanted to pick the colt up and hold him steady, but his legs would never get strong if I did. *I wonder if God feels the same way as He watches us struggle? Perhaps He holds onto the banisters of heaven and bites His lip as He leans over? Could it be painful for Him to see us bumble through life?* I'd never thought of God caring so much about me that it would hurt to watch me struggle. I'd grown through the adversity, and I wanted to continue to become a stronger person. I sighed. *Okay, God, I am ready to tackle this next season. Let it be the best ever.*

The colt switched his short black tail and pushed his front legs forward. Scooting his hind legs underneath him, he rocked forward and up on his front legs. Breathlessly I leaned forward. He heaved with his hind legs and stood, wobbling on all fours. Bobbing his head toward Snipe, he nickered, almost as if saying, "Mom, look at me!"

Ever since that day I've looked at my struggles differently. Instead of despairing over them, I embrace them, knowing God is watching over me. And when I get to the other side, I know I'll be a much better and stronger person.

> *Lord, please don't take the struggles away from me. Instead, strengthen my "inner man" so that I change into a better person as I conquer adversities. Amen.*

# 21

## God's Dream Horse

*Do what the LORD wants, and he
will give you your heart's desire.*

PSALM 37:4 CEV

The dirty dishes clattered as the waitress stacked them on her arm and carried them to the diner's kitchen. I sat in a red overstuffed booth scanning the "Horse" section of the classifieds in the *Missoulian*, our local newspaper. I wanted to ride my own horse, not an outfit horse. Over the last year I'd examined the newspaper every chance I had, searching for the right one for me. Most of them were too old or too young. I wanted a gelding between four and six years old that had some trail miles on him. Some of the horses advertised had injuries. Others had bad habits. Out of the dozens I'd ridden, I hadn't found any that fit. My last horse I'd sold in Virginia right before I moved to Montana. I missed having a deep relationship with my own horse.

Tracing my finger down the column in the paper, I mentally checked them off one by one. *You'd think in Montana it'd be easy to find a good saddle horse.* But it hadn't been. Worse yet, there wasn't a single prospect. I folded the paper into a heap next to my cup of coffee and sighed. *God, when am I going to find my horse?* It was already May, and soon the outfitting season would wind into full swing. Once it started, I wouldn't have a chance to shop around until December. That would mean another year without my own ride.

I glanced at my watch. *I better hustle.* I slid behind the steering wheel of the Ford pickup and glanced at my checklist. Before I drove the hour home and made dinner for the crew, I still had to stop by the vet clinic and get wormer for the horses and mules, pick up the saddles that had been mended at the saddle maker's shop, and get groceries—and that was just the top of the list. The pickup roared to life as I glanced at the next item. *Oh no! I told John I'd stop by when I was in town today. Why did I do that? I don't have time.* I moaned.

John had been a guide on last year's crew, and throughout the season he'd talked about the racehorse stud he had. He kept inviting me to stop by and see him. I groaned. *I don't care one whit about race horses,* I groused. When I thought of race horses I pictured hot temperaments that only had enough brains to fly out a gate and run until they killed themselves. The horses I was interested in used their agility and brains to figure out how to safely navigate mountain trails. I'd put John off all winter, but during our last conversation I'd finally agreed to stop by.

After zipping down the aisles of the grocery store, piling three shopping carts full, paying for them, and packing them in the truck, I drove to the vet clinic. I picked up the medicine and hopped into the truck. I glanced at my list and then my watch. *How am I going to get all this done and stop by John's? Maybe I'll call and tell him I'll see him the next time I'm in town.* While at the saddle shop, I thought about using the phone. *No, I need to swing by because he's a friend,* I decided.

An hour later the truck tires sloshed through the puddles in John's drive. He invited me in and, sitting at the kitchen table with a steaming cup of coffee, he leaned back in his chair and ran his hand through his sandy-brown hair as he excitedly showed me the stud's pedigree. I glanced under the table to look at my watch and stifled a yawn. Finally he stood and said, "Let's go take a look at him." I traipsed beside him through the barnyard.

As we strolled into the short row of outdoor paddocks, he listed the first horse's bloodlines. Stopping at the next one, he pointed at a newborn colt suckling on its mom. Its short, curly black mane danced as he butted his mother's udder. I stopped and gawked. Although John kept talking, I didn't hear a word he said. My attention was on that colt. He wiggled his rear, switched his tail, and slurped. Turning loose of the teat, he backed up and then stepped next to his mother's shoulder. She nuzzled his deep-reddish-brown coat. I couldn't take my eyes off him. There was a golden glow about him. Slowly he stretched, arching his neck and then his back. He turned his head and nonchalantly looked at us. A small white star dotted his forehead. He batted his long, black eyelashes. My heart skipped a beat. Then I reasoned, *Rebecca, you always like babies. Remember, you want a horse to ride this year.*

John turned and walked toward the stud's pen. Like a robot I followed. John scratched the stud's neck, and the big horse leaned into his fingers and closed his eyes, enjoying the attention. While John recounted the stud's accomplishments, I nodded my head and mumbled "uh-uh" at the right moments, but I wasn't really paying attention. I was enchanted with that colt. After a few minutes, John patted the stud's shoulder and asked, "So what do you think?"

My thoughts snapped back. "He's a dandy all right. Would you mind if I petted the colt on the way out?"

When we slipped into the colt's paddock, it wandered over to us and curiously smelled me. Holding out the back of my hand, I felt like I was in a dream. My heart raced. The whiskers on his muzzle tickled when he nosed my fingers. I reached for his neck and scratched his velveteen coat. He tipped his head sideways, asking for a harder scratch. I dug in for a minute and then patted his neck and ran my hand down his back. I walked around him taking inventory. He had four sturdy, straight legs. His left hind foot had a white sock. I knew this colt was mine. We watched him scamper around the paddock a few laps and then I asked, "Is he for sale?" John nodded and grinned. After shaking hands on a price, we agreed that I'd be back in a year to pick up *my* colt.

I chewed on my lip as I slid behind the steering wheel. I had peace inside, knowing God had led me here. Even though I hadn't been looking for a colt or for a race horse, God knew what was best. My mind drifted through of all the qualifications on my list of "what I want in my dream horse," and this colt only fit a couple of them. My heart sank. I knew where the difference came in. I'd been looking for what I wanted, but I hadn't asked God what He wanted for me.

The next May the tires on the pickup sloshed through the puddles when I drove down John's driveway to pick up my yearling I'd dubbed Czar.

Czar *was* my dream horse! After he was trained, he carried me safely over thousands of rugged mountain trails. Together we faced everything from grizzly bears to forest fires. He was the best and most trusted mount I'd ever ridden. Through God's still small voice leading me directly to Czar, I discovered that God's answers are much better than what my "dream" lists contain. Now after I define what I want, I add to my prayer, "And God, lead me to what You want for me."

*Lord, give me the fortitude to follow Your direction, especially when it's different from where I plan to go. Amen.*

# 22

# Drip, Drip, Drip

*Stay alert! Watch out for your great enemy,*
*the devil. He prowls around like a roaring*
*lion, looking for someone to devour.*

1 Peter 5:8 nlt

A coyote's howl drifted through the frosty, moonless night. A dozen head of horses and mules stood munching hay from the mangers in the wooden corral at Monture Camp. Fluffing the pillow under my head, I rolled over in my brown sleeping bag and the wooden cot sagged. A light breeze rattled the door flap of the canvas tent. Groping for my digital alarm clock, I pushed the snooze button so the time glowed: 12:01. My tummy growled and I groaned.

It was the first week of June, and four of us were in the hills setting up base camp. The days were long and so physically demanding that even though I ate constantly to keep my weight and energy up, I'd already lost nearly 20 pounds. I didn't have any more to lose. My 30 x 36-inch shrink-to-fit Levis were sagging. The worst part was that I knew I wouldn't be able to go back to sleep until I got something to eat. The closest food was all the way across camp in the cook tent. I snuggled into my sleeping bag. *It's too cold to get up.* Most springtime evenings in these mountains dip to freezing. My stomach rumbled, sounding like thunder.

I quickly unzipped the sleeping bag, stomped into my tall irrigation boots, and pulled on my winter jacket. Grabbing my flashlight, I switched it on and strode behind the beam to the cook tent. Shivering from the cold, I pulled a jar of peanut butter off the shelf, a knife out of the silverware drawer, and a loaf of bread out of the wooden bread box. I grumbled as I slathered the peanut butter across the bread. *That's a dumb rule.* I shook my finger at the sandwich as I said, "Thou shalt not eat in thy tent." *It'd be so much easier just to have some food in my tent, on the log by my head. Then all I'd have to do is roll over, pop it into my mouth, and go back to sleep.* My mouth watered as I gouged a bite out of the sandwich and chewed. *It's because of bears. But I haven't seen one track yet.* I stuffed another bite into my mouth, and then another. After dipping a cup into the water bucket, I washed down the last bite and packed the groceries away. Rubbing my hands together to warm my fingers, I stumbled back to my tent. In a few minutes I drifted to sleep.

Two hours later my tummy gurgled. My eyes popped open. I rolled over a couple times trying to go to sleep, but finally I gave up. I tramped over to the cook tent as I rubbed my arms and shivered. I ate and went back to bed. Two hours later my stomach groaned again. I walked like a zombie to the cook tent and back again. When the sun smiled golden rays from behind the mountain, I pulled the sleeping bag over my head. I was exhausted. I felt like I hadn't slept all night…and then my tummy growled.

The wood cookstove belched smoke as I lit the fire and tossed together a big breakfast for the guys and me. After stuffing down a stack of pancakes, eggs, and several sausages, along with a few cups of black coffee, I washed dishes while the guys saddled the horses and mules. They stuffed chainsaws and gas into the pannier bags on the mules. After saddling Sunrise, a palomino mare, my saddle creaked as I stepped up. We headed a half mile down the trail to cut wood for camp. I kept a close eye on the trail, watching for bear sign.

Chainsaws whined as the guys dropped trees and bucked them into four-foot logs, which we hefted onto the mules and tied to the packsaddles. I led the mules to camp, unloaded the logs, and took the mules back for load after load. Midday, between shuttling the logs, I stuffed down two roast beef sandwiches, a granola bar, and a Butterfinger candy bar. By three in the afternoon, while hauling the last load of logs in for the day, I leaned over and patted Sunrise's soft neck and whispered, "Did you see any bears? I didn't. I don't think it'd matter if I took food into my tent, do you?" Sunrise perked her ears and listened to me. "Just a bite or two wouldn't be a big deal, would it?" I straightened. "No, I better not," I said regretfully.

Once we got back to camp, we unsaddled the stock, stacked the logs into piles, ate dinner, and the last chore we did that evening was to tack a thick sheet of clear plastic over the top of my white wall tent. The plastic protected the tent so no rain would leak through the canvas and later on it would help the snow slide off.

Before crawling into my sleeping bag, I stopped by the cook tent and tanked up on groceries. Two hours later my tummy rumbled. My eyes popped open. I rolled over, and a blast of cold air rushed down my sleeping bag. I pulled it over my head. *I don't want to go over to the cook tent. I bet the folks who started the "no food in your tent policy" didn't have to get up in the middle of the night to eat. I'm different. I have to eat.* Slipping my feet into my boots, I clicked on my flashlight. *Maybe I could bring a little something back with me. Nothing smelly like peanut butter. Besides, who would know?*

I shrugged on my jacket and headed across camp. *Maybe something like granola. I could put it in a Ziploc bag. Surely no bear could smell that.* I rifled through the wooden kitchen boxes for the granola. *Besides, I need some sleep, and if I take some to my tent, I can just roll over instead of having to get dressed and trudge all the way here.* I poured some granola into a plastic bag and filled my water bottle. Smugly I hiked back to my tent following the dancing flashlight beam.

My cot groaned as I sat on it. I placed the granola and water bottle under the head-end of the cot. I shucked off my boots and jacket and wiggled into my sleeping bag. I zipped it up and fell asleep with a grin on my face. I woke up a couple times that night, rolled over, ate, and fell back to sleep. In the morning I sat on the edge of the cot and stretched. *Having that granola nearby was slick. I slept almost all night. I feel like a new woman.*

All day we cut trees and hauled logs. That evening when I slumped onto my cot, I had a bag of granola in one hand and a water bottle in the other. I tucked them underneath my cot and fluffed my pillow. Relaxed, I rolled into bed, knowing I was going to sleep like a baby.

A clap of thunder woke me up. The wind picked up and roared through camp, making my tent door snap wildly. I could hear the trees groaning. Lightning flashed across the sky, casting eerie shadows through the tent wall. Suddenly the sky cut loose and rain pelted down. *I love listening to storms, especially from inside a warm, dry sleeping bag.* I snuggled deeper into the sleeping bag and drifted off to sleep.

A few minutes later I felt a cold drop of water run down my neck. *How can that be? I must be dreaming.* Another drop hit me and dripped down my neck. Groggily reaching my hand up to check, I discovered the material over my head was soaked. I pushed the sleeping bag away from my head and rain spattered from the ceiling. *What is going on? Why isn't the plastic sheet keeping the rain out?* Quickly I crawled out of the sleeping bag and flicked on the flashlight. The roof of the tent was sagging under a puddle of water that was seeping through. I dragged my cot to the other side of the tent to keep it dry.

Puzzled, I stomped on my boots, shrugged on my jacket, and pulled on my cowboy hat. I slipped out the canvas flap to take a look. Casting the beam on the tent, I gasped. All the plastic above where my head had been was shredded. Huge, muddy paw prints were plastered on the side of the tent. Water dripped off the brim of my black hat as I stared at the bear tracks that lined the ground. My heart pounded in my ears. *When did this happen? Earlier when we were away from camp?* My mouth felt dry. *Or just now?* I swallowed hard. *Is the bear in the bushes watching me?* Slowly I shined the flashlight beam through the trees next to the tent. Nothing moved. I slipped back into the tent. The cot squeaked as I crawled into my sleeping bag. But instead of lying down, I sat up and wrapped my arms around my knees.

*What do I do now? I don't want to put the granola back in the cook tent because I might run into the bear. But I don't want to leave it in here either.* I rocked back and forth as my mind sifted my thoughts. *Oh, why did I bring the granola in here in the first place? I was told not to have food in my tent. But I couldn't sleep, and my tummy was rumbling. And it was going to happen again and again.* I chewed on my lip. *But that isn't the real problem.* The problem was that instead of allowing myself to be guided by a "commandment," all I'd focused on was how to get around it. I'd lost sight of the fact that the rule was put into place to protect me.

I traced the downward spiral. First, I'd entertained the thought of disobeying. After meditating on that for a while, I rationalized that a little food wouldn't matter. And then I added the "and who would know?" Besides, it was a dumb rule. Next, I justified that I was different, so it shouldn't apply to me anyway. And the convenience of having the granola in the tent would let me get more sleep, which was more important than following a stupid rule. After I disobeyed, I smugly thought that having it in my tent worked well for me.

I'd invested so much time into manipulating and massaging my thoughts into making it look okay, that I'd convinced myself that it was. The only problem was that the bear didn't care what I believed. He prowled around looking for food, and it was in my tent. By giving in to disobedience, I'd set myself up to be the victim of a bear attack. I squeezed my eyes closed. *This isn't any different than disobeying God. As soon as I do, I open myself up to the devil's schemes.*

The rain eased. I listened for sound—any sound—outside. The forest was still. The rest of the night I sat up on my cot, waiting, listening, and thinking. The bear never came back. The next morning I cleaned every crumb from my tent.

I haven't kept food in my tent since. There have been times when

I've been tempted to ignore a "thou shalt not," but then I remember that cold and scary night and come to the conclusion that even a little bit of disobedience is too much.

*Lord, thank You for giving me commandments to guard and protect me. Help me to look at them from Your point of view. Amen.*

# 23

# Fourth of July

*They speak of the glorious splendor of your majesty—*
*and I will meditate on your wonderful works.*

PSALM 145:5

The hot afternoon sun blistered the tan earth. Under the shade of tall, lodgepole pines, a row of sweaty horses and mules stood tied to the rope corral. They switched their tails and stomped their feet, trying to fend off the buzzing horseflies. The crew unsaddled the mules while the guests dug their lunch sacks out of their saddlebags. Amarillo, my copper-colored saddle horse, leaned into my fingers as I scratched his neck. "In a few minutes we're going to turn you loose, and you'll get to go roll in the dirt." I loosened the cinch, slipped the saddle off, and lugged it over to the stack of saddles. As I turned, I nearly tripped over Jeff, a 10-year-old guest. With twinkling green eyes he asked, "Do we have fireworks to celebrate the Fourth of July?"

"No, we can't set them off in the wilderness because of the fire danger."

His smile faded, and he lowered his eyes. I ruffled his sandy-brown hair. "You wouldn't want to start a forest fire, would you?"

Jeff shrugged his shoulders and answered in a monotone, "I suppose not."

My heart sank as I walked over to the kitchen. Not a breeze stirred as I stood next to the wood cookstove and flipped pork chops on the griddle. Sweat rolled down my back as my mind drifted back to my childhood.

The Fourth of July had been one of my favorite holidays. I grimaced. Jeff lived in the city, and he was used to big celebrations on Independence Day. *God, I feel awful. I didn't plan anything special for the guests. But what can I do now?*

All through dinner Jeff picked at his food. After eating, we built a campfire and roasted marshmallows. Jeff participated but mostly he stared at the coals.

The sun slipped lower in the sky, and a breeze rustled the leaves on the cottonwood trees. Billowy clouds lined the horizon. Shafts of golden rays streamed across the sky. The wind blew a strand of hair in my face. I tucked it behind my ear. The clouds marched across the sky like ranks of soldiers. Ribbons of pink light glowed from the bottom of the clouds, while the tops of them turned inky blue. An iridescent orange radiated across the sky followed by vibrant red.

Suddenly the clouds snuffed out the sun and everything became dark. One finger of lightning streaked across the sky. I glanced over at Jeff. With his eyes wide, he peered upward. The heavens rumbled. A gust of cold wind blasted through camp. Our kitchen tarp snapped and ballooned. The guylines pulled taut. A bolt of lightning zigzagged overhead. Another streamed across and then split into several shafts. *Crack!* Thunder clapped. A network of lightning bolts danced across the sky. They crisscrossed like a spider web, followed by ear-splitting peals of thunder. For the next half hour the sky exploded. I'd never seen a lightning show like it. Thunder rolled and clapped. Even the boulder I sat on shook. Before one streak of lightning ended, several more lit up the sky. Thunder boomed continuously. God was putting on His own laser light show.

As quickly as it started, the clouds marched away, leaving behind a crystalline-blue sky. I grinned at Jeff.

His green eyes twinkled as he watched the clouds fade away. He looked at me.

I nodded. "I think that was God saying, 'Happy Fourth of July, Jeff!'"

*Lord, the wonders of Your hands never cease to amaze me. Thank You. Amen.*

24

## Tag's Groaning

*Welcome people into your home
and don't grumble about it.*

1 Peter 4:9 CEV

In the meadow, the guests sipped their steaming hot coffee while seated around the bright-yellow folding tables. They visited as they finished the last bites of French toast, sausages, and eggs. Under the blue kitchen tarp I knelt in the cool grass next to a wooden box. I pulled out two loaves of bread and set them on the serving counter before pulling out and opening a jar of peanut butter. A gray jay, a bird nicknamed "camp robber," flew into the pine next to me and squawked. Ripping off a piece of bread from the heel, I tossed it toward him. "There you go, you little beggar." He snatched it and flew to a higher branch to gulp down his breakfast.

I glanced at my watch: eight o'clock. *Not a breeze in the air,* I noted. *It's going to be a scorcher today.* I pulled off my prickly wool sweater and draped it on the branch of a pine tree. I wanted to get the kitchen packed up and loaded onto the mules. The sooner we jumped into the saddle and headed down the trail, the sooner we could set up our next camp. And I wanted to be off the trail before we sweltered under the 100-degree or so temperature. Cupping my hands next to my mouth I yelled over to the guests, "Time to put in your lunch orders!"

Bob gathered his dishes and strolled over to the kitchen.

I pulled out four slices of bread and looked at him. "What'll you have?"

He pushed his heavy-framed glasses up his nose. Tipping his head back, he peered at the spread of lunch meats, chips, candy bars, breads, and condiments that lined my wooden kitchen box counter. "I'll take one PBJ with butter on white bread; one turkey with mayo, mustard, lettuce, tomato, cheddar cheese, and hot peppers on whole wheat; an Almond Joy; and some Cheez-Its."

The rest of the guests lined up behind him. No two orders were alike. One wanted Miracle Whip and another mayonnaise. *I'll be here till the moon rises getting all these special orders made,* I thought. *What a pain.* By the time I closed the last kitchen box, the wranglers had the guests' duffels mantied and were loading them onto the mules.

The guests stood by in awe as the crew quickly dissembled the kitchen—the folding tables and chairs, wooden kitchen boxes, counters, and the woodstove. All were mantied into matching loads, one pack for each side of the remaining mules. White canvas packs dotted the meadow when D.J., a wrangler, led over a tall, rawboned mule with a tan spot over his left eye. D.J. handed me the lead rope so I would hold Tag while he slung packs onto the packsaddle. Snugging down his tan cowboy hat he said, "I'm thinking the biggest mule should carry the heaviest load today."

I nodded.

The guests chattered and watched as D.J. walked over to the packs that held the woodstove and the meat packer. He grunted as he lifted the stove and placed it six feet away from the meat packer. I led Tag between the two loads and stopped. D.J. loosened the sling ropes on either side of the saddle. He picked up one end of the woodstove load and rested it on his knees. Then he bent over and grabbed the top end and lifted. The whole load now rested on his knees. He heaved it onto the saddle. Tag groaned—a long, pitiful groan that lingered in the air.

I giggled and rubbed Tag's neck. "You big baby." Suddenly I noticed the guests had become quiet.

D.J. tied the load in place and went around to the other side. He swung up the meat packer load and placed it on the saddle.

Once again Tag grooooooaaaaaaannnnnned.

Bob, the guest who'd put his lunch order in first, fiddled with his glasses. He looked up and asked with concern, "D.J., how heavy are those loads?"

D.J. chewed on his reddish-brown moustache. "I suppose 125 pounds each. Not much for a big ol' mule like this one." D.J. turned and walked off to fetch his saddle horse.

I finished tying off the sling ropes and turned to Bob. "It doesn't matter what we load on Tag, he always groans like that. Even if it only weighs a few pounds. He's so big, I don't think he can tell the difference."

Bob raised one eyebrow and rubbed his dark, stubbly beard.

I led Tag toward the string of mules and hollered over my shoulder, "I'll tell you what. Tomorrow we'll put a light load on him and you'll see."

The next morning the heat sweltered through the meadow where we were camped. After wake-up calls, I poured coffee for the guests. When Bob carried his dishes to the kitchen I jotted down his special order for lunch. I growled under my breath and tapped my pencil on the notepad as I looked up at the line of guests. *Why can't two of them have the same thing? This is ridiculous.* Buttering a slice of bread, I looked up at Bob. He stared at me as if to say something…and then he shifted his weight. I tipped my head, inquiringly.

He shyly asked, "So what are you loading on Tag today?"

I pointed the buttery knife toward a pile of boxes. "The empty cardboard kitchen boxes." I slathered jelly on a slice of bread. "Mantie tarp and all, they'll weigh under 15 pounds each."

Bob nodded.

I chuckled. "I guarantee Tag will groan just as loudly as he did yesterday." I stuffed the sandwich into a plastic sandwich bag, "He loves to groan whether it's a lot of work or just a little."

I froze. Is that what I'm doing? Groaning about making some silly sandwiches? So they all like different things. What is an extra 15 or 20 minutes? I glanced up at the guests standing in line. They chitchatted with each other, excited about another day of adventure. Placing the rest of Bob's lunch into his lunch sack, I scolded myself, *For goodness sakes, Rebecca, we're in the middle of the wilderness. It's not like they can run down to McDonald's to get something else. I want these people to have a special trip, and the extra effort I put into their lunches is a great place to start.*

After the crew took down the kitchen tarp and finished lining out the loads, the guests crowded around Tag. Making a show of it, D.J. picked up the mantied *empty* cardboard boxes with one hand. Balancing it on three fingers, he set it against the D-ring of Tag's packsaddle. As soon as it touched the saddle, Tag issued a long, drawn-out, pitiful groan. The guests burst out laughing.

I patted Tag's neck and under my breath said, "You got my attention through Tag, God."

*Lord, soften my heart to those around me. Show me ways I can help them feel special. Amen.*

# 25

# The Cliff!

*We demolish arguments and every pretension that sets
itself up against the knowledge of God, and we take
captive every thought to make it obedient to Christ.*

2 CORINTHIANS 10:5

The green banker's lamp glowed on my desk, where I sat with my chin propped on my hands. A gust of wind blasted through the open window. The strong breeze caught the papers on my desk. Quickly I slapped my right hand on them, and with my left I slid the window closed. Thunder rumbled and lightning flashed across the checklist of horses and mules the crew needed to catch tomorrow for the next summer trip. I circled Amarillo, my saddle horse.

*I really need to train Czar.* My gut twisted. Czar was my two-year-old bay gelding, and we were headed into the high country. I chewed on the pencil eraser. We'd be riding rocky trails that barely clung to the edge of cliffs. Even though I'd ridden in the high country a couple of years now, I'd never gotten used to the heights. I was petrified to ride along the craggy ledges that hung over sheer drop-offs. I'd been raised on the prairies of Minnesota where the only bump in town was scarcely big enough for snow sledding.

Tapping my pencil on Czar's name, I mumbled, "Riding the high country on a young horse." I shook my head. *What would he do if we ran into something scary on a narrow trail? Would he take off like a bullet? Or would he rear up, pivot, and run the other direction?* I twisted a strand of long blond hair and tucked it behind my ear while recalling stories of horses rearing up, losing their balance, falling over backward, and goring their riders with saddle horns. I wiped my sweaty palms on my jeans. *Do I really want to ride Czar?* But it was already August, this was the last summer trip and my only chance to put some miles on him this season without risking ice. I erased the circle around Amarillo and marked Czar's name.

The next morning a cloud of dust swirled around the pickup as it bounced down the dirt road. My stomach flip-flopped again when I thought of the narrow, craggy trails and Czar's lack of experience. Earlier that spring I'd sacked him out and ridden him a tad, but the summer trips had been so full I hadn't had a chance to work with him since. I pulled into the end-of-the-road. A cool summer breeze rustled the waist-deep grass as the crew bustled around saddling the mules. I saddled the guest horses and packed loads onto mules.

Apprehensively I tossed a saddle on Czar and tightened the cinch. He didn't flinch. After bridling him, I slipped my foot into the stirrup, threw my leg over the saddle, and settled in. He turned and batted his long, black eyelashes at me, as if we did this every day. As a precaution, I handed Czar's lead rope to the boss so he could pony us the first segment of the trail.

We rode out. Hoofbeats drummed on the hard-packed trail. The boss rode his bay Arabian gelding in the lead, then came Czar and me, followed by a long line of guests on their horses. At the end, two wranglers each pulled a string of mules. We splashed across Monture Creek, and the trail wound through a forest of enormous old larch trees. Czar's head bobbed as he calmly walked along. Bravely, I took the lead rope back.

The hot sun climbed into the sky as Czar nonchalantly picked his way down the trail. My heart pounded as I looked ahead. The canyon narrowed...and so did the trail. A steep slope rose on one side of the four-foot-wide trail, and the other side dropped into a canyon 50 feet below. With white knuckles I gripped the reins. In my mind I saw Czar step off the cliff, and we tumbled to the bottom. I swallowed hard and pulled Czar to a stop. Stepping out of the saddle I reasoned, *I'm not going to fall off a cliff because of an inexperienced horse.*

I led Czar until the trail widened and then I hopped back on. The next eight days, even though Czar performed like a champ, I led him across every narrow ledge. I couldn't get past the movie I'd made in my mind of us dropping off a cliff. I'd replayed it so many times that it had become real. I could even hear the rocks crashing down the mountain beside us.

The last night all the guests and crew sat around a crackling campfire. Smoke swirled and firelight flickered across our faces. We told stories and laughed about our adventures. I poked a stick into the fire until the end caught. Lifting it up, I turned the stick and watched the dancing flame.

Bob, one of the wranglers, tipped back his brown cowboy hat and teased, "When are you going to get on that horse and ride him all day? He's going to be fine."

Embarrassed, I stabbed the stick into the fire. *I am acting like a dude.* I looked up and faked a grin. "Tomorrow."

The next morning the sun rose hot and dry with a light breeze that rattled the leaves on the cottonwoods. My spurs jangled as I walked over to Czar and slipped on his bridle. The guests stuffed their lunches into their saddlebags and mounted their horses. My mouth was dry as I reined Czar to the lead. *Why did I say I'd ride Czar across the cliff today? Remember that nasty spot?* Instantly the horror movie played in my mind.

I shook my head and glanced behind me. The long line of guests meandered through the cottonwoods, followed by the pack strings. The trail followed the river through the bottom of a narrow canyon. Midmorning my stomach churned as Czar chugged uphill. The trail was funneling to only a couple feet wide. I wiped my sweaty palms on my jeans and tightened the reins. Ahead, the trail climbed up the side of the mountain and then wound around it. I cringed as I thought of the stretch where it traversed a shale rockslide and seemed to cling by a thread over a rushing river.

Czar lazily plodded along. I glanced down. The river pounded over boulders. The narrower the trail got, the closer Czar walked to the outside edge. My throat tightened. Stones dislodged from under his feet and clattered down the steep slope. *What's wrong with you, Czar? Can't you see it's straight down?*

The movie of us tumbling down the cliff clicked on. I tightened the reins and pulled Czar toward the mountain. Fear laced its icy fingers around me. My heart pounded. I inhaled shallow breaths. Czar lumbered around the bend. His hind foot slipped off the trail, pitching me forward in the saddle. Frantically I grabbed the reins and growled under my breath, "Watch where you're going!" I yanked him to the center of the trail.

Czar sauntered a couple steps and then drifted to the outside rim of the trail. I felt the blood drain out of my face. My eyes darted down the cliff. "Stop it!" I commanded.

I reached down to grab the reins tighter, but all I caught was air. Czar had stepped off the cliff—and into nothingness.

We fell—straight down. In a free-fall, I grabbed the saddle horn. *Wham!* Czar's feet crashed into the shale about a dozen feet down. My body slammed into the saddle. The impact drove the air out of me. I clung to the saddle with both hands.

The shale crumbled under his feet and clattered down the slope.

We skidded sideways down the cliff another five feet. Rocks crashed down the mountain and bounced into the rushing river below. Even though the cliff seemed straight down, Czar managed to skid to a stop.

I held my breath and didn't dare move for fear we'd tumble the rest of the way down and into the river.

I rolled my eyes up. The trail was way over my head.

The right side of my body was toward the cliff. I glanced down my left leg, past the stirrup, and saw the river pounding over boulders directly underneath. I couldn't see anything under Czar's feet. It was as if he stood on an invisible shelf. *This could give way at any second. I don't want to get trapped underneath him. I've got to get off!*

I glanced at the slope for something to grab on to—a bush, a branch, anything. Nothing. And the slope was too steep for me to step off. I wouldn't be able to get a foothold in the shale. I'd only fall down the slope, possibly under Czar's hooves.

The pounding of the river entombed me. I glimpsed down my left stirrup again. It was a long way down. If we slid again, there wasn't anything to stop us. The momentum that we'd gather going down would crush us into the boulders. And waves of shale would probably break Czar's legs before we hit bottom.

Several rocks under Czar's feet broke free and wildly bounced into the river. I gritted my teeth. *God, help me!*

Czar braced his legs, but we started to slide.

My mind whirled. There was only one thing to do if we were going to live. I yanked on the uphill rein. At the same time I pulled my legs away from Czar's body and then slammed my spurs into his sides. Czar had never been jabbed with spurs. Shocked, he heaved uphill. When he pushed off with his rear legs, the rocks he'd been standing on crashed down the mountain.

Czar scrambled for footing. Everything under his feet slid. His legs churned.

I pulled the uphill rein and slammed him with my spurs again.

He heaved himself up and then tried to brace himself as we slid downhill…backward.

I gathered all my strength and pounded him with the spurs. "Don't stop!" I yelled. He leaped uphill, his feet scrambling for footholds. Sweat poured down his neck. He panted.

Spurring him on, Czar heaved again. And again. He clawed his way to the top and wrestled his body over the edge and onto the trail. A landslide of rocks we'd just stood on crashed down the slope and plunged into the river.

Czar hung his head low, gasping for air as he trudged along the narrow trail. White lather foamed down his neck and shoulders. My heart pounded and my hands shook. Briefly I closed my eyes and breathed a sigh of relief. Slumping, I loosened the reins and looked at the trail in front of me. The steep shale hillside rose straight up on my right side. In 50 yards the narrow ledge of a trail rounded the side of the mountain and dropped through a creek before widening out onto a flat, pine-studded bench. I couldn't wait for level ground!

My body swayed with each of Czar's steps. Suddenly Czar swung his head up. He snorted and jumped to the right, toward the cliff, throwing me off balance. I grabbed the saddle and gasped as he reared up and pivoted 90 degrees to the right. Dropping his front hooves onto the steep shale, he plunged uphill. Rocks clattered down the mountain.

He lunged again and again. The slope was so steep that his weight tipped backward. He teetered, his front hooves barely able to dig in. Rocks flew down the slope.

I grabbed Czar's mane closer to his head and threw my weight toward the cliff—trying to push his front feet to the ground. *God, help me!*

Sweat poured down Czar's neck. He panted and clawed for footing. He stood vertically on his hind legs. We hung like a pendulum. Then his body tipped backward. An alarm sounded in my head. *Get your feet out of the stirrups!* I kicked my feet free just as we somersaulted down.

In midair, with all my might, I pushed away from the saddle. I tucked into a ball and tumbled down the cliff. Czar crashed below me onto the trail. Then everything was still.

I lay prone on the cliff. Rocks stabbed my back. I groaned, rolled over, and stiffly slid down to the trail. Czar stood up, shook, and then walked to the nearest clump of grass and started eating.

The guests rode around the bend, clinging to their saddle horns in fear and staring at me. In unison they yelled, "Are you okay?"

I gritted my teeth and hissed, "I will be after I grab that horse." Dusting myself off, I stormed for Czar. He glanced at me, snorted, and trotted away. Cornering him on a switchback, I grabbed his ears. With laser-beam eyes I glared at him and growled, "If you ever do anything that stupid again—even the slightest itsy-bitsy thing, you'll be dog food!"

I grabbed the reins and stomped down the trail. With each step my mind replayed the horrific scene. Both of my greatest fears had happened within minutes of each other. *Why? God, I don't understand.* Deep in my spirit I heard, *I commanded you to fear not.* My spirit was pierced by the words. For several years my fear of heights and flipping off cliffs had consumed me. My boots scuffed down the dusty trail. My back and legs were so sore I could barely lift my feet. The sun beat down on us, and sweat trickled down my back. I stopped, threaded the reins around Czar's neck, set my foot in the stirrup, and swung my other leg over the saddle. *But, God, even though I believe in You, my fears happened like I imagined they would. I'm confused.*

Overhead a raven circled and cawed. The trail threaded through the tall pines and then it narrowed. My heart thudded. My body stiffened. *I will not fear...I will not fear.* Czar picked his way across the rocky ledge. Cold sweat drenched my body. The full-color motion picture of falling off the cliff assaulted my mind. Czar drifted to the outside edge.

I shook my head to clear the thoughts and then realized that out of fear I was leaning toward the uphill side. When I did that, my pelvis tilted down on that side and pushed Czar away—toward the drop off. *That's why he kept drifting to the outside rim!* My fear had programed my body to create the exact thing I'd focused on. I had sabotaged myself into falling off the cliff. I'd ignored God's command to "fear not" and put my faith in Him. Instead, I had dwelled on my fears so much that I created the movie in my head and then helped live it out. I'd developed faith in my fear...and fear was faith in the devil.

Armed with my new knowledge I rode across the next cliff. It was torture. As soon as Czar's hoof dislodged a rock and I heard it tumble down the slope, cold fingers of fear choked me and turned on the motion picture. I forced myself to put a sliding stop on those thoughts. I concentrated on sitting centered in the saddle while Czar casually walked across the cliff. I kept repeating, "I refuse to fear. God will take care of me." I wrestled with terror the whole way. Across the next cliff section and then the next. Each time, I corralled the thoughts of fear and replaced them with thoughts of God. Eventually it became easier. By the time we reached camp, the fear had evaporated.

That day Czar taught me a valuable lesson: When thoughts of fear run rampant in my mind, I need to toss a loop over them and turn them toward God *before* they have a chance to program me for failure.

I rode Czar thousands of miles over narrow, craggy trails, and he never stepped off another cliff. Praise the Lord!

*Lord, arrest my spirit when I place faith in fear. Give me the courage to trust You to keep me safe. Amen.*

# 26

# Back to Camp

*A person's wisdom yields patience;*
*it is to one's glory to overlook an offense.*

PROVERBS 19:11

A squirrel scolded from the top of a lodgepole pine and knocked a lump of snow off a branch. Some of it fell onto my shoulder. I brushed it off and pulled down my Elmer Fudd cap. Zipping up my winter jacket to block out the frosty morning breeze, I centered my weight in the saddle. Czar carefully picked his way down the steep, rocky slope. Five horses and one mule made up the string I was leading down the mountain.

Earlier this morning, long before daybreak, I'd ridden out of camp with four hunters and two guides. Only a couple stars twinkled as we rode miles through the pitch-black morning, up a steep mountain trail and into a small grassy meadow under the rocky lip of Limestone Pass. When we got there, a faint blue light glowed from the horizon where the sun was going to come up. Saddles creaked as we all dismounted. Each guide set out with two guests to hunt down the mountain and back to camp. It was my job to lead the stock back. I'd tightened cinches and tied the stirrups on top of the saddles so they wouldn't get hung up on branches and brush. Then I tied the stock together single file. Normally I loved this ride, but not today. Steam rose from my breath into the frigid air as I mulled over an encounter with one of the guests.

Behind me I could hear the clattering from the hooves of the five horses and mule as they navigated the narrow trail. Every stem of grass and every needle on the pines was encrusted with hoarfrost. In my heart, I was frosted as I replayed the events of dinner last night. Yesterday afternoon I'd ridden the 14 miles into camp ahead of the guests so I could have a hot dinner waiting for them. The cook tent smelled of tacos, refried beans, corn, and Mexican rice. Grated cheese, salsa, and tossed salad were on the buffet counter. I'd just finished dishing up individual servings of strawberry shortcake when the guests strolled into the cook tent. Their eyes bugged out at the feast that was waiting—all except Greg's. He was a short, fine-boned man who strutted as if he were the one who had created the universe. Greg had been on two other pack trips with me this season. Each time I met him, he was a bigger bully than before.

With his nostrils pinched, Greg ran his hand through his black hair. He squinted his eyes, lifted his chin, and announced, "I don't like tacos."

I leveled my gaze with his and replied, "I guess you'll be hungry for breakfast." Turning away, I stuffed a log into the cookstove. It belched smoke.

Even now, hours later, my blood boiled. *He knows we pack the exact amount of food needed for each trip. It's not like I can drive down the road and get him something else from the grocery store. How rude! Wouldn't a nice person keep his mouth shut and pick through the food, eating around the tacos? But he's not nice. He did that to humiliate me in front of the other guests.*

I gritted my teeth and pulled down the scarf that was over my mouth. The steam from my breath had made it wet. *It's going to be a long hunt.* I shifted my weight in the saddle and turned around to check on the stock. The horses trudged in step with each other, and the saddles rode centered. I frowned. Minnesota, the black mule with the white nose, casually strolled along too, but his lead rope was dragging and there wasn't a saddle on his back! *How can that be? I tightened the cinch. How did it come off? Where could it be?*

I stopped, slipped out of the saddle, and tied Czar and the lead horse to a tree. I walked back and grabbed Minnesota's rope. Leading him to the horse in front of him, I scolded, "Minnesota, what did you do with that saddle? Now we have to go find it." I tied him on the back of the string. Then I untied Czar and the lead horse, hopped into the saddle, and, turning the string around, backtracked.

Scanning the trail in front of me, my mind flipped through my tallies against Greg. His first trip with the outfit had been on a black bear hunt. The guide had driven him in a pickup to some of the best hunting areas, but once there Greg refused to get out and walk. He insisted on staying in the truck and then whined when he didn't fill his tag. Our brochure stated that strenuous hiking was to be expected if a hunter wanted success. I shook my head. *How can anyone please a guy like that?*

The sun popped over the hill in front of me. The frost on the pine needles instantly melted and dripped from the boughs overhead. I shivered as a drop slithered down my neck. The trail rounded a bend, and there it was—the huge, square-skirted saddle in a heap in the middle of the trail. I climbed off Czar and tied him and my lead horse to a tree. I went back, untied Minnesota and led him to the saddle. I wagged my finger at him and said, "Now you stand still while I saddle you." Brushing off the saddle pad, I tossed it onto his back. I grunted as I picked up the heavy leather saddle and tossed it up. The antique western saddle felt like it weighed as much as I did. I cinched it as tight as I could and then shortened the straps to the breast collar and the crupper. I led Minnesota to the end of the string and tied him to the last horse. For good measure I rechecked the cinch and pulled it two notches tighter. "That's not going anywhere now."

Untying the lead horse and Czar, I climbed into the saddle. I nudged Czar into a walk. The string and I wound through the pines. By the time the horses's hooves broke the ice on the edges of the bog, my thoughts were deeply mired in the offenses I'd tallied up against Greg. This past summer he'd come on a fishing trip. I remembered him stomping over to the river with his fly pole in hand. I'm sure his stomping scared away every fish within 200 yards. He peered over the bank and announced, "I don't see any fish. There aren't any fish in this river!" Then he turned on his heels and stormed away. He never did try to catch anything. My saddle groaned as I turned to glance at the stock behind me. They lolly-gagged down the trail. I squinted. Minnesota was back a ways, cropping grass. When he saw me looking at him, he trotted to catch up, his lead rope trailing behind him. And there wasn't a saddle on his back!

After tying Minnesota to the saddle of the last horse in the string, once again we backtracked in search of the saddle. It lay in a heap. This time when I saddled, I waved my finger in Minnesota's face and scolded, "Bad mule! You're supposed to keep that saddle on your back." I cinched the saddle down so tight I thought his eyes would pop. I tied him on the end of the string again, hopped back on Czar, and we wound down the mountain.

A light breeze whispered through the pines. The trail turned downhill, and so did my thoughts. *How am I going to manage the next eight days with Greg? I wish I could pack him up and ride him right to the airport.* Czar shifted his weight onto his haunches as he half walked and half skidded down a steep section of the trail. Rocks clattered down the slope as the string skidded along behind us. The trail leveled as we rode into a small meadow. I glanced back to check the horses and Minnesota. The mule's head came up. He pricked his long ears forward and craned his neck as he looked at me, as if saying, "Watch this, Mom!" I gawked as he curled his body into a sideways "C." He flipped his tail out of the crupper, lowered his head, and then wiggled his shoulders until the saddle fell over his head. Minnesota beamed like he'd just given me a blue ribbon performance.

I vaulted out of the saddle. "Bad mule! You're a bad mule!"

Minnesota blinked as if he couldn't believe I wasn't impressed. During the next ten minutes while I saddled him, I lectured him about proper mule behavior. Taking one last tug to tighten the cinch, I snipped, "You've got some learning to do, mister."

And deep in my spirit I heard, *So do you.* I gasped, but before I could gather my thoughts, the still small voice bubbled up inside. *You need to learn to shuck offenses as easily as Minnesota shucks his saddle.*

My heart sank. I'd gotten mired down in offenses against Greg. Worse yet, I'd been continuously rehearsing them and had been wallowing in bitterness. Indirectly I'd been letting Greg control my attitude. I wasn't acting any better than he was. I smiled as I thought about shucking an offense. I could see Greg hurling insults at me and me ducking while the insults hurled past—all the while smugly thinking, "Take that devil! I'm not touching that with a 10-foot pole."

The rest of the ride back to camp I concentrated on *not* thinking about Greg. Minnesota kept shucking his saddle, so I finally tied it into sort of a ball and loaded it on top of one of the horses.

That evening, out of the leftover tacos, I made chili for our dinner soup. I had to smother a giggle when Greg dished up a big bowl, dipped in his spoon, and with a mouthful said, "Great chili." The rest of the hunt he was a bully, but I didn't take the bait. Instead I concentrated on enjoying the other guests.

That hunt I learned a valuable lesson: I don't have to pick up an offense; I can choose to shuck it off instead.

*Lord, help me to duck and shrug my shoulders so I won't get tangled in bitterness. Amen.*

27

# What? No Winter Pasture?

*Take the yoke I give you. Put it on your
shoulders and learn from me. I am gentle
and humble, and you will find rest. This yoke
is easy to bear, and this burden is light.*

MATTHEW 11:29-30 CEV

October's golden sunlight filtered through the white canvas of the kitchen tent. I sat at the plank table chewing on a pencil eraser while reviewing the list of horses and mules. Dawn's cool breeze rolled off the mountain and through the tent, making the canvas door flap gently. I walked over to the corner woodpile, pulled out a chunk of split wood, and stuffed it into the stove. It belched a small cloud of smoke, and then the fire crackled and popped and roared to life. Sitting on the weathered wooden bench, I frowned. *In a month and a half, 60 head of horses and mules will need winter pasture. Where am I going to put them?*

Every December when the outfitting season rolled to a close, the herd of working stock would be trucked to winter pasture. Only the pregnant mares and yearlings would stay at the ranch and be fed hay through the winter. The day before I'd ridden into camp for this hunt, I'd gotten a phone call informing me that the winter pasture arrangements had fallen through. My stomach had been churning ever since.

*Where am I going to find pasture? It's not like everybody has hundreds of acres to spare.* I groaned as my mind raced through possibilities. The pasture needed to be close enough that we could safely truck the stock in December over snowy roads. It needed to be located in one of the few "banana belt" areas of Montana where the snow never gets too deep the critters could forage for food. Those spots were few and far between.

I nervously tapped my pencil. *And how am I going to find pasture when I'm out here—14 miles into the wilderness with no phone?* I fretted as I thought about my schedule. I was the cook for every 10-day hunt until the season was over. I would be riding out for two days between the hunts, but in those days I shuffled guests to and from the airport, bought and packed groceries, did laundry for crew, and took care of a long list of details for work and me. *Besides, I don't know a soul who has any available pasture.* I rubbed my forehead. *And if I can't find pasture, it'll cost about $12,000 for hay. No way we want to pay that!*

The sound of voices and the clatter of hooves drifted down the mountain, interrupting my stampeding thoughts. *What are the hunters doing back so soon? They just left!* I walked over to the door where my jacket hung on a peg next to the stove. Slipping into my wool coat, I walked out the door.

Bob nodded and reined Hazy Joe, a brown Arabian mare, toward me while the guests rode to the hitching rail by the tack shed. I rubbed Hazy Joe's shoulder as Bob spoke under his breath. "I came in because Saul's not able to climb the hills." I glanced toward the hitching rail where a guest was tying up Saul, a lanky brown thoroughbred who was the newest horse in the herd. Bob continued. "He wasn't able to keep his footing going up the steep stuff. I figured it'd be better to swap out horses than to have a wreck."

I nodded and replied, "I'll check him over after you leave."

After watching them get another mount ready and disappear up the hill, I grabbed a curry comb out of the tack shed. Leaning against the hitching rail I eyed Saul's young and lean body. I'd bought him two months ago. His owners had raced him on the Montana horse racing circuit. When he didn't prove himself, they'd discarded him at an auction yard. When I'd seen him in the corral at the stockyard, I'd raised my eyebrows and thought, *He looks like a good mountain horse: high enough withers to hold a saddle, a deep chest for good lung capacity, long straight legs, and soft, kind eyes.* Besides, he looked too good to go to slaughter.

I was pleasantly surprised when I brought him home and he melded into the herd as if he'd always been with them. When I rode him on a summer trip, I understood why he washed out of racing. He didn't have any competitive drive; instead, he enjoyed walking down the trail behind another horse and loved getting attention from his rider. I immediately put him in the "dude string." The guests loved him.

Setting the blue plastic curry comb behind his ears, I stroked down his neck. He leaned into the brush as I softly spoke to him. "So, buddy, are you going to let me know what's going on?" I finished brushing his body but didn't find any sore spots. "Why couldn't you climb the mountain?" I asked.

I set a saddle pad in place and tossed up the saddle. He didn't flinch when I pulled the cinch tight or object when I slid a bit into his mouth. He didn't even goose when I slipped my leg over the saddle and snuggled in. Gathering the reins I eased him away from the hitching rail and nudged him into a fast walk.

Ravens squawked and drifted overhead as we wove between the white tents. Finally I pushed him into a trot. Leaves rustles and twigs snapped under his feet as he smoothly floated around camp. I drew him in. "Okay, let's try the hill."

The "hill" was actually the foot of a mountain that rose straight out of the ground behind camp. After rising nearly vertically for 100 yards, it leveled into a small basin before gradually sloping a few miles to the peak. I turned Saul up the trail. Instead of scrambling up the hill by powering from his haunches, he threw his weight forward. Before

I could stop him, he frantically ran, chugging and clawing with his front hooves. Rocks dislodged and clattered behind us. I gasped as he hopped, lunged, and pawed. We hung vertically, and then his weight tipped, almost as if he were going to summersault backward. I stretched forward over the saddle horn, arching my body toward his neck. I pushed my feet into the stirrups behind me, leveraging all my weight over his shoulders so his front feet would stay on the ground. In a few leaps he topped the rise. We stopped.

My heart pounded and I sighed. "I can tell you've never been in the high country," I told him. I glanced around the small grassy basin looking for a gentle rise where I could teach him how to shift his weight to use his haunches as his power base.

A fall breeze whispered through the pines. To my left, on the south side of the mountain, a short but steep rise looked perfect. I turned Saul and we sauntered toward it. Stopping at the bottom, I reached down and petted him. "So, Saul, you normally carry 65 percent of your weight over your front end, but things are different going uphill."

I nudged him forward. He took one step and shifted his weight over his front feet. I drew him in, and shifted my weight toward the back of the saddle. To compensate, he automatically shifted his weight to his rear. I rubbed his neck. "Good boy," I encouraged. His ears swiveled as he listened to me. Over the next half hour we practiced going up one step at a time. Finally Saul quit shouldering into the hill and walked uphill by powering off his haunches.

Rubbing my forehead, I turned him toward camp, my mind back to the pasture problem. *What can I do about the pasture?* While Saul carefully picked his way down the trail and off the foot of the mountain, my thoughts chiseled at my heart. *How am I going to come up with $12,000 for hay?*

I reined Saul around some pine trees and then headed back up the steep trail. Instead of using his new skills, he shouldered into the slope. I pulled him to a stop and scolded, "Remember, it's not that hard. Your front end wasn't made to carry all your weight uphill." When

I said that, I heard a still small voice from my spirit say, *You weren't made to carry all the weight either. Shift your weight onto Me.*

"But how can I do that, Lord?" I countered. "I've got to find pasture." A warm presence engulfed me as the inner voice said, *Quit focusing on the problem and believe that I will help you.*

After a dozen times up the steep hill, Saul climbed like a pro. Over the next several days every time negative thoughts pierced me I'd say, "God, I'm shifting the weight of this onto You. I'm not going to think about finding or not finding pasture until I'm out of the hills where You and I can do something about it." A couple times I wiped my sweaty palms on my jeans and had to repeat my determination over and over again.

At the end of the hunt I rode into civilization. After getting the stock and gear settled, I drove to the post office. As I stepped out of the Ford pickup, a friend and a fellow outfitter pulled up in her blue van. She stepped out and we hugged.

Karen asked, "How's your season going?"

I shared the news from our camp and then added, "Our winter pasture plans fell through, so if you hear of any pastures available, would you let me know?"

Karen nodded. "We're taking our herd up to the Indian reservation. You might want to talk with Jack. I think there's room for yours too."

A quick phone call to Jack confirmed Karen's thought. The Indian reservation wasn't in a "banana belt," but it was in an area where the wind kept the prairie swept clean of snow and yet had gullies that would provide shelter for the horses and mules. Problem solved!

That phone call bolstered my belief in God. When I quit focusing on my problem and shifted the weight onto God, together—as a team—we worked everything out.

> *Lord, when I'm worried, please remind me that we have a yoke that stretches between us. Thank You for shouldering the heaviest part of the burden. Amen.*

28

# Snowflakes

*You are worthy, O Lord our God, to receive glory
and honor and power. For you created all things,
and they exist because you created what you pleased.*

REVELATION 4:11 NLT

Thick gray clouds hung like a blanket over the canyon, blocking the snowcapped peaks from view. Although it was midday, it was as dark as it would be right before sunset. The crisp air nipped at my cheeks. It smelled like fresh snow was on its way. My saddle moaned as I snuggled down inside my winter jacket and looked ahead with a blank stare. My bay saddle horse's hooves crunched through the snow. It was a ho-hum kind of a day. The next four hours I'd ride the 14 miles into hunting camp alone so I could get into camp ahead of the guests and have hot soup waiting for them. I yawned. The outfitting season was winding down for the year, and everything was going along smoothly. I'd ridden this trail so many times I was a tad bit bored and felt like I was on autopilot.

Czar trudged just over three miles an hour through the familiar stands of pines. We skirted the same hillsides, the only difference being that the pine boughs now sagged with snow and the rocks were hidden from view. My body swayed monotonously with each of Czar's steps. My mind drifted. I felt gray like the clouds; not happy, not sad, just…

there. I tapped the end of the reins against my chaps. Glancing at my watch I sighed. *Another two hours to go.* A light breeze picked up and whispered through the pines. Chunks of snow fell from the branches, creating staccato sounds through the forest.

A squirrel chattered from a branch overhead as snowflakes lazily drifted from the sky. They piled up on my shoulders and on Czar's mane. The air was white, thick with flakes that gradually grew larger until they were the size of quarters. A light wind whirled them in circles. An enormous snowflake rushed toward my face and stuck to my eyelashes. It tickled. I giggled and with a gray woolen mitten carefully scooped it off. While cradling it close to my face, I stared at the multitude of miniature crystals stuck together to make one snowflake. *And no two snowflakes are alike,* I remembered. I looked at the millions of snowflakes that floated down, some clinging to branches, others falling to the ground. I tipped my head back, opened my mouth wide, and stuck out my tongue. The ice-cold crystals prickled. I smiled and swallowed.

Holding a mitten in front of me, snowflakes clustered in the wool fibers. The clouds overhead parted just a crack, and a few rays of sunshine beamed. They glittered off the flakes, and each prism radiated different colors. Some were golden, others glowed green, pink, and blue. *All the colors of the rainbow are contained in one snowflake,* I thought. I moved my hand and the snowflakes sparkled. *That makes sense. A rainbow is nothing more than droplets of water reflecting light. And rainbows contain a promise from God.* Breathlessly I scooped snowflakes off Czar's mane and held them next to my face. I felt as if I were holding priceless promises from God in the palm of my mitten.

In awe I watched them melt into droplets of water. Each droplet looked the same. *Why would God bother to make each snowflake different only to have each one melt and disappear?* The snowflakes danced on the gentle breeze, swooping and twirling to the music of the wind whispering through the boughs. It was as if they were rejoicing. My heart skipped. They were messages of love from God. A God who cared so much that He created each snowflake unique—just like He created each person unique.

I tipped my mitten, each crystal of the snowflakes catching the light and bursting forth with rainbow-colored lights. *Each light reflects God's love. He created these for me to enjoy.* I was looking into the heart of God and into the depth of His love for me.

I shook the droplets off my mittens. *This beauty was here all along, but I didn't see it.* When that snowflake landed on my eyelashes, God opened my eyes. It was almost like He put a pair of special glasses on me—"God spectacles"—so I could see the beauty He created. Joy danced in my heart and chased away the gray ho-hums.

Czar's hooves swooshed through the snow. I leaned back and rode the rest of the way into camp in awe of this world that was frosted with the glittering promises of God. I glanced through the forest at the fresh, white ground. The sunshine made the snow sparkle like a sea of diamonds between the deep-green pines. God's creation was shouting His love.

*Why have a gray day when I can turn it into an incredible day?* I decided. Now when I'm feeling ho-hum or blue, I put on my God spectacles and marvel at the magnificent details God created for me to enjoy.

> *Lord, when I have gray ho-hum days, please open my eyes to see Your glory and Your love. Amen.*

29

# The Capital "H" in Horsepower

*Our people must learn to devote themselves to doing
what is good...and not live unproductive lives.*

TITUS 3:14

A gust of wind rocked the two-ton stock truck. I grabbed the steering wheel, hunkered down, and peered out the windshield. The snow blew sideways, drifting in the long driveway to the ranch. I'd just hauled a load of horses to a different pasture and was headed home to change clothes and then go off to a meeting this afternoon. My holiday season commitments rolled through my head. The outfitting season was winding down, but I would stay busy because I was deeply involved in community and professional organizations, church, and the lives of my friends. Coming up this month were Christmas parties and outfitter conferences. The hardest part was my friends knew I was out of the hills so they were calling to catch up. Other people called about projects I was working on. I was delighted to receive every call, but as soon as I started in on a project, the phone would ring, reminding me of something else that had to be done. So I'd skip to the next thing. Piles of half-completed projects littered my desk. *How can I get everything done on time?*

Fog etched its way across the windshield, and I flipped the defroster on high. The wind howled across the road. Even though I squinted, I could barely see through the snowflakes. An outline of a drift was in front of me. I accelerated, and the truck barreled ahead. It hit the drift, and the chains on the rear tires clattered as they dug in. The engine roared and the truck chugged through. But as soon as the tires cleared that one, the truck smacked a deep one. Snow flew against the windshield. The tires groaned. The truck bucked. I felt the rear end sinking as the tires spun. Then the back end slid a foot off the right side of the road. Quickly I let off the gas and groaned. *How frustrating. I'm almost to the house.*

The hinges protested as I pulled the door handle and leaned against the door. I jumped down and glanced at the rear tires. They were sunk in snow deeper than the axle. I groaned again. *What's big enough to pull this tank out?* I rubbed my forehead. *The only thing that's bigger is the county plow.*

I grabbed the scoop shovel from behind the seat and started digging. With each shovelful the storm subsided until only the wind blew. I got one of the dual rear tires dug out. Hearing tire chains rattling up the drive, I looked up to see Ted rolling down the window of his older pickup.

"Looks like you might need some help."

Ted lived next door, and he occasionally worked for the outfit as a guide. Pulling his Elmer Fudd hat over his gray hair, he shut off the truck and grabbed a scoop shovel out of the back. For a short, wiry cowboy, he sure could dig. I barely got the second tire scooped out before he had both of the others cleared.

I hopped into the truck and rolled down the window. Ted stood back as the engine roared to life. I shifted into low gear. Slowly I eased out the clutch. The tires spun and the truck's rear end tipped further into the ditch. A couple days before we'd had freezing rain, so there was ice under the snow. The left tires were spinning while the right ones slipped.

Ted waved his arm, making a cutting motion across his throat. He stepped up on the running board and hung onto the mirror. "Let me hook up my truck. I'll try pulling you out."

I nodded but as he walked away I rolled my eyes. *There's no way his one-ton truck can pull me out.* I sighed. *He's just doing it to be nice.*

Ted maneuvered his truck in front while I dug out the tow chain from behind the front seat. I hooked it on the frame of the stock truck and connected it to his truck. With both of us behind steering wheels, Ted flipped his thumb up. I "thumbed up" in return. He slowly pulled forward, taking the slack out of the chain. When the chain was taut, my truck rocked forward.

I eased down on the gas pedal and up on the clutch. His truck's rear end hunkered down. The stock truck shook; its tires spun. Suddenly Ted's truck lost traction. The tires whined against ice. We both let off the gas.

Over the next ten minutes we tried every which way to get that truck pulled out but nothing worked. Finally Ted hopped out and walked over, rubbing his chin. "I'm going to get my stud horse. He's got caulks on his shoes. He can pull this truck out in no time. I'll be right back." He unhooked his truck and zoomed down the driveway.

I huddled in the stock truck warming my hands over the heater. Hopelessly I shook my head. *There's no way. How can his horse pull it out if his one-ton truck couldn't?* The two-ton stock truck was enormous—and that was before the boss had it customized with steel stock panels that lined the bed. I had no idea what the truck weighed, but I knew it was tons.

I'd seen Ted's stud horse. He wasn't very big. *I bet he doesn't even weigh a thousand pounds.* I tapped my fingers on the steering wheel. All fall I'd listened to Ted tell stories about that stud and his horse-logging adventures. Ted would yarn on and on about the brute strength of that critter. Oftentimes I'd nod my head and yawn, sure that he had embellished the stories into tall tales. I felt sorry for Ted. That horse was his pride and joy. *He's going to hang his head when the stud can't budge this truck.*

I looked in the rearview mirror to see Ted, wearing his red-and-black plaid wool coat and sitting atop his harnessed horse, coming down the driveway. The stud was coated in snow and ice except where Ted had chipped it away for the harness. I rolled down the window while he trotted past. The truck loomed over that horse.

Stopping the horse in front of the truck, Ted slid off his back. I rolled my eyes. *There's no way. That stud's nose doesn't even clear the hood.*

Ted tugged down on the lead rope, motioning the horse to stand still. My neighbor hooked the tow chain to the harness and then stepped up on the running boards of the stock truck. He poked his head through the open window and told me to shift it into neutral.

I faked a grin and nodded.

Standing in front of his stud, Ted bowed his head and shrugged his shoulders. He wiggled his feet, almost like he was withdrawing inside himself. Then he grasped the lead rope. The horse leaned its head into Ted's chest while Ted rubbed its ears and talked. Over the loud engine I couldn't hear a word of what he was saying, but it was almost as if that stud understood what Ted was telling him.

Ted stepped to the side. Holding the lead rope at arm's length, he tapped it. The stud stepped forward to take the slack out of the harness. When it was taut, the horse stopped. He shifted his weight back and forth as he planted his hind feet. A chunk of snow fell off his back. Then he leaned forward in the harness. Ted wiggled the rope, and the stud dug in with its shoulders and hind legs. The truck moved an inch. The stud held his ground, but the truck didn't budge more. Ted released the rope, and the stud relaxed. Ted flashed me a toothy grin and hollered, "Just had to show him what he was in for."

I grinned and nodded. *Uh huh*, I thought.

Ted stroked the stud's neck and talked some more. They seemed to be in a huddle. Then the man stepped aside. Taking the slack out of the lead rope, he looked the stud in the eye. His horse picked up its left hind foot and shifted it into place. Then its right hind leg shifted.

The beast crouched and then bowed its neck while settling its shoulders into the harness. It leaned forward.

Ted nodded and the stud buckled down. Chunks of ice fell away as the horse's muscles bulged.

The stock truck groaned and rolled forward a couple of inches.

I held my breath.

Every muscle in the stud was rigid. The harness was stretched so tight it looked like it might snap. The stud stared straight ahead and bore down.

It seemed like hours, but it must have been just seconds. The truck wiggled ahead several more inches.

My heart raced. *Can that little horse really pull out this gargantuan truck?*

The stud's nostrils flared wide. It stood its ground, breathing hard. It crouched lower and pushed into the harness. The truck rolled forward a foot.

I bit my cheek and looked in the rearview mirror at the back tires. A sense of awe swept through me. Suddenly I was overwhelmed with desire to see this underdog win. I slapped the steering wheel and yelled over the growl of the engine, "C'mon. You can do it!"

Ted stood by the stud's side, quietly encouraging him. The animal's muscles quivered while he dug in his hooves. With each deep breath, his rib cage expanded and contracted. His muscles rippled from his shoulders through the top of his back and down his legs.

I leaned forward and gripped the steering wheel even tighter.

With his whole heart, the stud plowed into the harness and dug the caulks of his shoes into the ice.

The truck protested with creaks and groans. Suddenly it shuddered and rolled free.

Ted danced by the stud's side. The horse relaxed and arched its neck and rolled his shoulders, relieved to be free of the weight. It wiggled its rear and shook. Ted bounced as he slapped his horse's neck and shouted, "Yahoo! I knew you could do it!"

I set the emergency brake and bounded out of the truck. In awe I walked next to the amazing horse. Sweat rolled down his neck. With nostrils flared, he nodded his head and asked for a scratch on his forehead. I dug my fingers into his sweaty brow and said, "If I wouldn't have seen it, I never would have believed it. You are some horse!"

Ted rubbed its neck and looked me in the eye. "Do you know why he was able to pull that truck out?"

I shook my head.

"Because he has an incredible ability to focus," Ted said. "Did you see how once he buckled down, he never eased up? He held his ground until the truck moved. Now that's the power of focus."

I thanked Ted, and he proudly scrambled on top of the stallion. I watched him ride out of sight.

*Maybe all those stories Ted told about that stud were true.* I stepped up into the truck and bucked it through the last few drifts in the drive. Walking into the house, I looked at my stack of half-finished projects. *I can learn something from that horse. God has given me the ability to focus too. It's time to buckle down and zero in on one thing at a time until each job is finished. And no distractions allowed, such as answering the phone.*

After that day, if Ted would have told me he was going to use that stud to pull down the Empire State Building, I would have bought a ringside seat. That horse put a capital "H" in Horsepower.

> *Lord, thank You for introducing me to horses who teach me how to succeed. Amen.*

# 30

# Wiggles

*I no longer call you slaves, because a master doesn't*
*confide in his slaves. Now you are my friends, since*
*I have told you everything the Father told me.*

JOHN 15:15 NLT

Dawn's light filtered peachy rays through the scattered thin clouds. The spring mountain air, carrying the fresh scent of snow from the high country, gently brushed my cheeks. Two pregnant mares nuzzled me as I latched the gate. They were hoping I had grain. I scratched their necks. "You mooches. You'll get your grain later." I turned toward Star, who stood five feet away. Her three-day-old filly pranced by her side. The filly was nearly a carbon copy of her dam: a sorrel with a star on her forehead, long straight legs, and a couple white socks. She bowed her neck as she stared at me. Her short red mane stood on end in a row of miniature ringlets. The air was so cool that steam rolled from her nostrils, leaving droplets of moisture on her whiskers.

Star nonchalantly nibbled the frosty grass and drifted away. The filly bobbed her head as I stepped toward her. She glanced over her shoulder at her mom and then switched her fuzzy red tail and danced to the far side of her mom.

Star lifted her head as I walked toward her.

"That's a beautiful, strong baby you have. Do you like being a mom?" She leaned into my hand as I scratched her forehead. "I've only got a few minutes, and I've got a whole list of stuff to do with your baby before you go out to summer pasture in a couple weeks." I rubbed Star's warm neck while moving toward the filly.

The filly lowered her head and stared at me. Slowly I lifted the back of my hand toward her. She sniffed me. I reached to pet her neck. She stepped back and I stopped. "What's wrong, little girl? Yesterday—and the day before—I petted you all over and you liked it. Don't you remember?"

The filly batted her long, red eyelashes and sauntered behind her mom.

Star plucked stems of grass as I rubbed her side and again moved toward the foal. As soon as I walked around Star's rear end, the baby skittered around Star's nose to the opposite side. I turned 180 degrees and attempted to step around Star so I'd be on the same side as the filly. Star pivoted, blocking me from her baby. Putting my hands on my hips, I stared at Star. "What's that all about? Did you do that on purpose?"

Star nibbled some more grass but watched me out of the corner of her eye.

I glanced at my watch. In five minutes I had to jump into the truck and head to Missoula. Over the next few minutes I tried everything I could think of to pet that filly, but I wasn't able to get near her. After the baby had been born, I guess hormones raced and maternal instincts kicked in, making Star extremely possessive. Basking in her mother's attention, the filly made up this game called "Stay Away from Rebecca." I'd raised several foals, but I'd never had this happen. Finally in disgust I threw up my hands, stomped out of the pasture, and roared away in the truck—outfoxed by a three-day-old.

The miles of asphalt hummed under the tires. *I've got a whole checklist of stuff I've got to accomplish with her, and my time's running out. I have to get her gentled before the other colts are born or I'll have a mutiny on my hands.* I methodically ticked through my checklist: catch her, touch her all over, pick up her feet, halter and lead her alongside her mom, get her used to ropes being draped over her back and legs. Mentally I put her on my own checklist for first thing in the morning.

The next morning I woke up with a plan. On the way into the pasture I dished up three pans of grain, stacking them on top of each other. I was greeted at the gate with loud nickers. Quickly I spread out the grain pans, placing one in front of Star last.

The filly danced. The morning sunlight glinted off her red, velveteen coat. Cocking her head from side to side, she watched her mom gobble the food. I rubbed Star's shoulder, focused my eyes on the ground, and spoke quietly to the filly. "Someday you'll like grain too."

The filly pricked her ears. I held out the back of my hand. Without moving her feet, she craned her neck to sniff me. I stood still and cooed, "Today you're going to learn all kinds of stuff." She relaxed.

I shifted my weight to turn toward her. The filly scampered to the opposite side of her mom.

I groaned. "Blast!"

I turned my back toward her and edged closer. I'd get within one step, and she'd squirt three steps away. This game went on and on until she finally drowsily leaned against her mom.

Looking at the ground, I eased toward her. "If you stand still, you can rest." I extended my hand.

She blinked, trying to keep her heavy eyelids open. I reached toward her shoulder. *Only a few more inches.*

Suddenly the filly exploded. She gathered her hind legs under her and took off running like a rocket—but only going as far as the opposite side of Star. Clumps of dirt from her hooves sprayed me.

Tears of frustration oozed out of the corners of my eyes. *God, what do I do now?* I turned to go to the other side of Star, and the toe of my boot caught on the heel of the other. Tripping, I fell forward and caught myself with my arms just before hitting the ground.

As I pulled myself upright I caught a movement out of the corner of my eye. The filly was peeking under Star's belly at me. I laughed.

Straightening up, I stood on my tiptoes and looked over Star's back. "Peek-a-boo!"

The filly looked up, seemingly shocked.

Quickly I ducked out of sight behind Star's belly.

I waited a few seconds and then squatted down.

The filly stared at me, sniffing curiously.

I chuckled and hid once again behind Star's belly.

Seconds later I heard the clatter of the filly's hooves as she slowly stalked behind her mom. She eased her nose and one eye around Star's rear.

I laughed. "So all it takes is peek-a-boo?"

Within my heart I heard, *No, not peek-a-boo. She doesn't want to be an item on your checklist. She wants a relationship. She wants to be your friend—to laugh and play with you. That's what I want too.*

A strange thought captured me. *Laugh? With God?* I'd always viewed God as prim and proper, rather aloof, and perhaps a bit tight-lipped. I'd never envisioned Him having fun...or laughing—especially with me.

Fear gripped me, and I worried that I'd misunderstood God. Hesitantly I asked, "God, how can that be?" Once again I sensed His voice: *I want to be your friend. Friends laugh together.*

The filly watched me, cocking her head side to side. She bobbed her head and scampered around Star. Leaning against Star, the foal butted her mom's udder and then suckled. I peeked underneath. The baby watched me out of the corner of her eye as she butted and slurped. Milk dripped from her chin.

*What would she like from me? Hmmm...I've never seen a colt that didn't like this.* I stood on my tiptoes, reached over Star's back, and gently scratched the filly's haunch. She slurped louder and sucked faster, but she didn't move away from my hand. I pushed a little harder as I rubbed. The filly quit suckling and backed into my hand, enjoying the massage. In a few moments she was wiggling her rear side to side like a hula dancer. I burst out laughing and wondered if God was chuckling as well.

Over the next few days I set the checklist aside. The only way that filly would let me touch her was by draping my arm over her mom's back and scratching her. Thus I became the "scratch machine." Eventually she let me walk behind her and scratch. Then I could stand by her side to scratch her. Finally I was able to walk up to her head. The filly earned the name "Wiggles," and I learned that relationships require laughter and playtime.

> *Lord, show me how to have a relationship where we laugh and enjoy life together as friends. Amen.*

# 31

# An Atomic Bomb?

*Teach us to realize the brevity of life, so
that we may grow in wisdom.*

PSALM 90:12 NLT

A lone hawk circled overhead, its shrill scream piercing the air as it hunted for a mouse scurrying through the grass. The spring sun felt good as it beat down on my bare arms. A light breeze whispered across my cheek. Reaching down, I patted the sweaty neck of my mount, the speckled cinnamon-and-sugar colored appaloosa named Melinda. She swiveled her ears back, listening to me chatter. "We'll be to the top in a minute, and you can take a long break there."

Snuffy, who was riding his big bay mare in the lead, topped the ridge, swept off his brown cowboy hat, and shouted, "Wahoo, this is beautiful!"

I grinned and nudged Melinda forward. Susan pulled off her cowboy hat, and her blond hair tumbled in the breeze. She slapped the hat on her horse's rear as both our horses heaved over the top of the mountain at the same time. I inhaled, filling my lungs with the sweet scent of pines as I glanced across the blue ridges that stretched as far as I could see.

We were out on a Sunday afternoon ride in mid May. Snuffy and his girlfriend, Susan, had planned a ride and invited me to tag along. They didn't have to ask twice. We saddled up and rode out from the ranch. After a few miles on the gravel road, we disappeared into the mountains. It'd taken us an hour and a half to get up here. I relaxed and enjoyed the view. The day couldn't be more perfect. We never guessed that in the next half hour we'd be shrouded in terror.

The three of us dismounted, tied the horses to trees, and dug through our saddlebags for our water bottles and lunches. Some downed logs littered the ground, and we sat on them, eating and continuing to enjoy the view.

Snuffy tucked the last bite of sandwich into his mouth. With the back of his hand he wiped his brown moustache. Pausing, he pointed to the west. "Look at that black cloud boiling in. We better ride down before the storm hits. If there's lightning we don't want to be on top of the mountain."

We hurried and were soon ready. I swung into the saddle. Turning Melinda, I noticed Snuffy, seated on his mare, was squinting into the distance. His face had turned ashen. I looked west, and then looked again. The black cloud was a lot closer. It was barreling toward us like a freight train and seemed to consume the whole horizon. Snuffy glanced at Susan and me. He kicked his mare and said, "Better make some tracks!"

Snuffy took the lead, then Susan, and I fell in behind. The next 20 minutes we pointed the horses down the steep, grassy slope. We leaned back in our saddles and pushed the horses as hard as we dared. By the time we reached the bottom, that cloud had blocked the sun. Even though it was only early evening, it seemed a lot later as the dark settled around us.

An ominous feeling overshadowed us. Nervously we watched the sky as the horses' hooves crunched down the gravel road that wound through a narrow, rocky canyon. The air grew hazy as if a fog had rolled in—but it wasn't fog.

Snuffy reined in his mare and waited for Susan's horse to walk alongside. I nudged Melinda into a trot to catch up. The three of us rode elbow-to-elbow. Snuffy chewed his brown moustache as he turned toward us. "This isn't a storm brewing—at least not a thunderstorm. But what is it?"

We stared into the sky. A few miniature flakes floated down. *Flakes?* It wasn't cold enough to be snow. The smell of something bitter stung my nose. I sneezed. The powdery stuff floated down thicker. Speckles of gray coated the trees, the road, the horses, and us. I frowned at my arm. Gingerly I wiped some away. Then I rubbed some between my index finger and my thumb. It looked like gray flour but had a heavier consistency.

My throat prickled. I coughed and swallowed, but the sensation didn't go away. My throat was burning. My mouth watered and the saliva ran down my throat. My heart raced. Whatever this stuff was, my body didn't want to breathe it. I cleared my throat. "Is this stuff burning your throats?" I asked.

Susan's face puckered as she nodded and coughed.

Snuffy swallowed hard and nodded before unbuckling his saddlebags and pulling a red bandana out. Immediately Susan and I did the same. The three of us shook out our bandanas, folded them in half into "V's," and tied them across our noses. We looked like old-fashioned bank robbers as we nudged our horses into a fast walk.

Susan untied her jacket from behind the saddle. Confused and scared, my mind tripped along. *Will this stuff burn our skin eventually?* My saddle groaned as I shifted and turned to untie my denim jacket from behind the saddle. Before I slipped it on, I tried to brush the gray stuff off my arm. It smudged. I shuddered. I'd never seen anything like this. *What's happening?* I squinted into the sky. I cleared my throat. My voice wavered as I asked, "What is this stuff?"

The horses hustled down the dirt road, their hoofbeats muffled by the accumulation of gray powder on the ground. Snuffy pulled on his brown Carhartt jacket and turned the collar up. He snugged down his brown cowboy hat. "The way I figure, there's only one explanation."

Susan and I stared at him.

The bandana over his mouth slipped down. He pulled it up and tied it tighter. "The only thing this can be is ash. That enormous cloud that rolled across the sky was from an explosion."

My throat burned. I tried to clear my throat. Coughing, I glanced at Susan. The bandana over my mouth muffled my words. "But the cloud filled the whole horizon! What would cause that large of an explosion?"

Our eyes grew wide. Together Susan and I chimed, "Could it be an atomic bomb?" Instantly I visualized sitting at a high school desk in history class watching films of an atomic bomb blowing up with the telltale mushrooming cloud consuming the sky. I felt the blood drain out of my face. *No, Rebecca! Get a grip. It couldn't have been an atomic bomb.*

I felt like I was caught in a nightmare and couldn't wake up. *Can this really be happening?* A light breeze swirled the ash that showered from the sky. Soon it was so thick that although Susan rode by my left elbow, I could barely see the outline of her body. The world disappeared under a cloak of gray. A piece of ash stuck in my throat. I choked and wheezed, trying to catch my breath. Saliva flooded my throat. I swallowed hard and gasped a breath, and then another.

Although the temperature was warm, the cold sweat of fear beaded on the palms of my hands. Ash stuck to them. My heart raced as I wiped them on my jeans. My mind clicked through the facts. We were an hour from the ranch by horseback, and there wasn't any shelter between here and there. Not a soul knew we were out here, so we couldn't count on anyone to come get us. There wasn't any way to contact anybody or hear a news report. *Will this stuff hurt us? How about the horses?* My body felt cold and stiff. *Could the ash be toxic? Could it be toxic fallout?*

I felt my saddle raise as Melinda took a deep breath, and then she coughed a deep, raspy cough. In a few steps Snuffy's mare coughed and then Susan's.

Snuffy reined in his mare. "We'd better slow them down or they might not make it home."

Every moment torturously ticked past. The ash dumped from a sky that was growing darker by the minute. Twilight neared. *How much more can possibly fall? Will it ever end?* Ash blanketed the road, and the powder muffled the only sound I could hear—hoofbeats and breathing. Every few minutes one of the horses coughed, and each time it grew deeper and raspier. We rode in silence, swaying in our saddles and lost in the terror of our thoughts.

The gray dust coated my eyelashes. My eyes burned from the ash. They felt sticky and dry. *I wish I could tune in a news report so I could find out what is going on.* I squinted, hoping my eyes would water and wash away some of the ash. *Will this stuff make me go blind?* My throat burned. *Could it kill us?* I gripped the reins with icy fingers. *How long will it take? Will it be painful?* My breathing shortened as my mind churned. *What could cause an explosion this big other than a bomb? Could there have been a mistake at a nuclear plant and it blew up? Or was it a bomb? Who would bomb us? A terrorist?* I felt like a prisoner in a mad scientist's experiment. I wanted to scream "Get me out of here now!"

Ash fell so thickly that I could barely see my hands. It drifted over the top of us and settled on everything. I slumped in the saddle. *It had to be an enormous bomb to produce a cloud that consumed the sky. Could another country have bombed us? Does that mean we're at war?* Drifts of gray piled on us. I brushed some from Melinda's straggly mane and then a pile from off my shoulders. *Why did I come on this ride? If I would have stayed home, I'd be inside and protected right now. Will we make it home?*

The sun fell over the horizon, extinguishing the last glimmer of light. Darkness strangled us. Moisture from my breath built up on the bandana, making the ash cling to it. That made the rag sag against my mouth and nose. *God, I feel like I'm being smothered to death. What can I do? Help me!* Bending over the edge of my saddle, I shook the loose edge of the bandana. The ash fell off in clumps. I coughed.

Melinda stumbled, throwing my body forward. I braced against the saddle horn as she fell on her front knees and then jerked back to her feet. Bracing her feet, she coughed and shook her whole body all the way to her tail. She coughed again. My body swayed as she stepped forward into the black night.

When Melinda stumbled, something rose up inside of me saying, *Follow Melinda's lead. Shake off the world and focus on taking one step forward.* Melinda had been focusing on the next step, which brought her closer to home. I'm sure she was scared. She probably hadn't ever seen anything like this. I'm sure she had a hard time breathing, and the stuff burned her lungs like it did mine. Yet she took one step forward into the darkness, and then another and another.

I'd been so consumed with thoughts of what might happen that I'd lost sight of this moment in time. I'd built a craggy mountain of uncertainties so high that I couldn't possibly scale it. The worst part was that I'd only meditated on things I couldn't change. I'd been tormenting myself with those thoughts, and it was sapping my strength.

The veil over my mind cleared. My thoughts whirled and sorted. *Was it a bomb? I don't know. Can I change the situation? No. So don't think about it anymore. Period. Ash is falling from the sky. Can I stop it? No. Can I do something about it? Yes—I put a bandana over my face. But what about Melinda?* I blinked and squinted. I couldn't see anything in the darkness. I knew we couldn't ease the burden on the horses by getting off and walking because we would lose our way. And I couldn't rig a bandana over her nose. *But I could wipe it out.*

In the dark, I reined in Melinda and said to Snuffy and Susan, "I'm going to check Melinda's nose."

They chimed in, "Good idea." Saddles creaked as we dismounted. Melinda stood still as I groped along her side and unbuckled the saddlebags. I pulled out another bandana and my flashlight. When I clicked the flashlight on, the beam barely penetrated the thick ash that drifted down like a blizzard. I stepped to her head and held the reins. Her warm breath whispered over my knuckles as I swabbed the pudding-like substance out of her nose. "There you go, girl." I scratched her forehead.

After the three of us mounted, we trekked down the road, stopping every 10 to 15 minutes to check our mounts' noses. Every time a horse coughed, a stray, negative thought tried to wedge into my mind. I chased each one away with a question: *Can I change it?* The answer was always no. *So stop thinking about it!* Finally the horses stopped by a hitching rail. We were home! We unsaddled. I shuddered when I turned Melinda out into the pasture. I looked at the horses and mules and wished I had a barn.

The wooden porch steps groaned as the three of us dashed to the door, dusted the gray ash off, and hurried into the house. I flipped on the light. Snuffy scrambled to the TV and Susan the radio. In a matter of moments we were shocked to hear that Mount St. Helens in Washington had blown her top.

*An active volcano in the lower 48 states? Like Pompeii? Weren't they just in underprivileged countries?* I chuckled. Somehow I'd missed volcanoes in Washington in my geography classes. None of the terrifying thoughts that had run rampant in my mind were true. I'd wasted my emotions and part of a day of my life focusing on wild imaginations.

The broadcast warned people to stay inside for a couple days and to avoid breathing the ash. Although it was hazardous, it wasn't toxic. By the next morning, drifts of ash 8 to 12 inches deep covered everything. The horses and mules all looked the same—gray from the top of their ears to the bottom of their hooves.

Snuffy, Susan, me, the horses, the mules—and probably every other living creature caught out in the ash—coughed until the next spring when our bodies finally cleaned themselves out.

That ash-covered day I learned a nugget of truth—one I took with me into the wilderness and one that saved my life many times over: No matter how small or how sensational a situation is, even if there's blood present, evaluate what's happening based on the information available at that moment in time. When trouble strikes, I start with the big picture and work down until I get to the level where I can do something constructive. After acknowledging the facts and praying, I focus on what I can change.

> *Lord, thank You for being with me through my adventures and for teaching me wisdom to live by. Amen.*

# 32

## *Rendezvous*

*Trust in your money and down you go! But
the godly flourish like leaves in spring.*

PROVERBS 11:28 NLT

The sun slipped behind the peaks, casting tall shadows across Dry
Fork valley. Melinda, the appaloosa mare with the rat tail, stood
picketed and lazily munched grass. Next to my saddle, I kicked rocks
out of the grass and threw them to the side. Shaking out my red sleeping bag, I nestled it into that spot and unlaced my leather boots. Pulling them off, I wiggled inside the sleeping bag. I took off my fleece
jacket, rolled it up for a pillow, and lay down. My stomach churned as
I watched the first star twinkle in the sky. *Am I doing the right thing?
Should I have quit my job to come back here?*

For the winter I'd been working as an optician at a mall in Missoula, Montana. Then Jack and Karen, friends who were outfitters,
called and mentioned they were looking for a backcountry cook. I
bailed out of the city job. Because I planned to attend a friend's wed-
ding, Jack and Karen had left on their first summer pack trip without
me, although they did take most of my gear. We planned to rendez-
vous "somewhere on Basin Creek," which was a stretch of river several
miles long and more than 35 miles into the Bob Marshall Wilderness.

Earlier today I'd witnessed my friend's "I do" and then jumped into my car. I zoomed to the trailhead where Melinda paced in the corral. Quickly I saddled and tied on my sleeping bag, hobble, picket, rope, and slicker. Opening my saddlebags, I tucked in some granola bars and my water bottle. By seven o'clock, I kicked Melinda into a trot. She was night blind, so at the first sign of twilight we'd have to stop. I wanted to make Dry Fork before lights out. We barely made it.

An owl hooted, and the sound floated through the valley. I plumped my fleece jacket, scooted it back under my neck, and stared into the cobalt-blue sky. Something inside my jeans pocket poked me. I dug out a wad of dollar bills. *I should have left these in the car. They're worthless back here. I can't even start a fire with them.* The paper money had absorbed the moisture in the air so they were so damp that if I tried to light them with a match, they wouldn't hold the flame. I stuffed the bills into a jacket pocket. Another star glimmered as I drifted off to sleep.

I awoke to dawn's first rays barely glowing over the peaks. Melinda lay sound asleep in the meadow. I glanced at my watch: four o'clock. I rubbed my eyes. Pulling the sleeping bag over my head, I rolled over. My mind rewound to last night's thoughts. *Why did I give up a year-round job for a seasonal job? There was only one answer. The only reason I was working at the mall was money.* Groaning, I tossed the sleeping bag aside and grabbed my boots. Melinda raised her head and glared at me. I chuckled. "Time to get up, sleepyhead!" She rocked to her feet and shook.

Golden rays of light shimmered over the eastern peaks. Within 20 minutes I slipped into the saddle and nudged Melinda into a trot. With the steady drum of her hooves, thoughts marched through my head. *The only place I feel at peace is in the hills. I feel like God created me to live back here.* I sighed. It certainly wasn't society's norm—especially for a girl. I felt pressured to "get a good job, grow up, and settle down." But year after year, when the snow receded in the spring, I longingly eyed the snowcapped mountains. Like a magnet I was drawn back into them.

The trail wound through meadows, dipped into creeks, and crossed gentle and steep slopes. I alternated walking and trotting Melinda. With each step, her hooves kicked up small clouds of dust. Mile after mile passed as my mind argued mountain job versus city job. The mountain job ministered to my heart. It felt so right! But every winter I pounded the pavement looking for a job to tide me over. *What am I going to do this winter?*

A mosquito landed on Melinda's neck. I swatted it. The city job made sense in my head. It was full-time, year-round work. The optician position was my first job with a "future." Sweat and dirt ran down Melinda's neck. We rode into Basin Creek. I reined her in and examined the dirt trail for tracks.

Nestled between the mountains, Basin Creek was at least six miles long. The edges of the lush meadow extended into the folds of the mountains. I'd never been on a trip with Jack and Karen, so I wasn't sure where they would be. I knew that they wouldn't camp on the main trail. Instead they'd bushwhack off the trail, maybe as far as a mile. They'd set up camp on the creek, tucked into one of the meadow's fingers.

Imprints of horse and mule tracks stamped the trail. The sun warmed my back as I nudged Melinda forward, keeping my eyes glued to the trail. A half-hour later the tracks ended. Along the left side of the trail, the grass was bent over. I smiled and reined Melinda off the trail. In a few minutes Melinda's chest swelled and she whinnied. In the distance mules honked and horses neighed in return. I kicked Melinda into a trot. We topped a small rise and trotted down the slope. Smoke from a wood cookstove lazily floated through the meadow, carrying with it the smell of coffee. My mouth watered.

Green tents dotted the meadow. Karen and Greg, a wrangler, were sitting next to the cookstove. Karen waved. They got up and walked through the knee-high grass toward me. Karen smiled and tucked a strand of gray hair behind her ear. "You're in early. It's only nine thirty. Did you have a good ride?"

I nodded and slipped out of the saddle. Karen turned to Greg. "Would you unsaddle for her?" He nodded so I handed him the reins.

Karen and I strolled to the cookstove. She filled me in on the happenings and mentioned that the guests were on a day ride. Her eyes twinkled as she poured a cup of coffee and said, "I just had a discussion with Greg. I told him that you'd be here any minute and asked him to set up your tent. He laughed at me and said, 'She won't be in this early—if she makes it at all.'" Karen chuckled again and handed me the cup.

The words struck me. I hadn't ever doubted that I'd make it safely and that I'd find them. I hadn't given a second thought to riding off with a sleeping bag, two granola bars, and a water bottle to meet friends who were camped 35 miles into the wilderness. And their given location had been merely a general area that encompassed several square miles. I had confidence in my ability in the woods.

Slipping my hand into my jacket pocket, my fingers stubbed the wad of dollar bills, *Why didn't I have confidence in my heart about taking the job?* I glanced at the ground. *It was because I had been putting my trust in the money of the city job.* I'd struggled with the city job because it made sense when I "looked" with my natural eyes at the money, but in my spirit I knew God wanted me to work in the mountains another season. The warring of the two viewpoints had made me miserable. *Okay God, I'm giving it to You. I'll need You to find me a job this winter, but I'm not going to fret about it now. I'm here in the woods doing what I love. I'm going to enjoy every minute of it! No more arguing in my head.*

> *Teach me, Lord, to base my decisions on where You're leading me and not on money. Amen.*

## 33

# *What's His Name?*

*A good name is more desirable than great riches;*
*to be esteemed is better than silver or gold.*

Proverbs 22:1

The diesel engine of the red-and-gray, three-quarter-ton Dodge pickup growled as it chugged up the mountain lugging the empty four-horse trailer. Topping the ridge we sailed down the other side, through the rolling hills and meadows dotted with thousands of cattle. I was on my way to pick up the horse I'd just bought. My heart fluttered as I thought of how perfect he would be for me. His previous owner had invested years into combining three breeds to create a powerful horse for mountain work and it showed. The one-eighth Percheron gave him heavy bones, the three-eighths TwoEyed Jack quarter horse lineage added a skip and athleticism to his step, and the half fox trotter lengthened his stride. I couldn't wait to load him in the trailer.

I rolled down the window. The July morning air carried the scent of fresh-cut alfalfa. I inhaled deeply as I glanced at the small herd of horses grazing among the cows. There were sorrels, bays, and blacks. I grinned as I thought of this horse's coloring. He was a paint horse with big blotches of dapple black, dapple gray, and white. The most unusual coloring I'd ever seen. I knew he was perfect. Well, almost. His owner had named him Quincy. It didn't fit him.

I drummed the steering wheel with my fingers. *What am I going to call him?* An animal's name was extremely important to me. I wanted it to be something that not only represented him, but something he could grow in to. With the nearly 100 horses and mules I'd owned in my lifetime, I'd used up most all the common horse names. Then I went on a Bible character binge and had named some Matthew, Mark, Luke, John, Obadiah, and the like. But this time I wanted something really unique, a name that only my horse would have. *Perhaps it could have a different spelling or contain a goal?*

My mind drifted to the first time I saw him in the pine-studded meadow. The tall, green grass waved in the breeze and tousled his long black mane and tail. The big white blotches of his coloring looked like clouds and the dapple black and gray made it look like a stormy sky. *That's it!* "Sky." No, that's too plain. *Stormy? No, one of my friends had a Stormy.* The truck tires hummed on the asphalt, and my mind chugged through possibilities. A question bubbled out of my spirit: *What do you like to do when you ride?* That was easy. My favorite thing to do was to pray. *And prayer is a song in the sky to Me.*

The breeze from the window fluttered my long hair. I tucked it under my collar and played with the words. "Song Sky…Sky Song. Hmmm, it's not two words…Skysong. No…not quite. How about SkySong? That's it!" It was a name to which we could both aspire. He would be my main mount while I spent time in the saddle with God.

*Lord, thank You for keeping my goals in front of me—all in my horse's name. Amen.*

34

# Pecking Order

*Surrender to God! Resist the devil,
and he will run from you.*

JAMES 4:7 CEV

From the branch over the barn, a robin chirped its morning song as I carried prickly flakes of alfalfa hay through the corral. The sun was still hiding behind the mountains, casting dawn's peachy tint on the thin clouds that lay in swirls against the July blue sky. I tossed the hay into the wooden feeder. Instantly Dazzle, my black Tennessee walker mare, bellied up and stuffed her mouth. SkySong, my new dapple gray-and-white gelding, sauntered to the opposite side of the feeder. As he reached his lips to grab flakes of hay, Dazzle barreled around the feeder. Pinning back her ears, she squinted her eyes into laser beams and rushed at Sky-Song. Innocently SkySong glanced at her as if to say, "Excuse me," and strolled to the opposite side of the feeder.

SkySong pulled some hay out of the feeder and munched. Suddenly Dazzle snorted, pinned back her ears, and thundered next to SkySong. She spun her rear toward him, hunched up, and let her hind legs fly—flinging dirt and rocks. Although she missed by a mile, her warning was clear: The next time SkySong ate out of the feeder she was going to nail him with both hind feet. SkySong bolted 10 feet away then looked at me as if saying, "What are you going to do about that?"

I threw my hands up. "Don't let her bully you like that. You're bigger

158

than she is. Stand up for yourself!" SkySong stared forlornly at the hay. I'd owned him for a week, but had kept him in a separate paddock next to Dazzle so they could get acquainted. Yesterday I put them together, and Dazzle herded him around and refused to let him eat. I kicked the toe of my boot in the dirt. *Why did I buy SkySong?*

Last fall I'd put down a deposit on an intensive horse training class which started in May. I'd been riding Dazzle in the class, and a couple weeks ago her joints swelled from trotting on the lunge line. Before we started, I knew that she had slight joint issues, but I thought she'd be okay. That wasn't the case, she showed signs of pain. Immediately I quit riding her. I was heartbroken. It was my dream class. I'd invested a large chunk of money and six weeks of my time. I didn't have another horse I could use. *God, I thought you wanted me to take this class. What do I do now?*

The next few days during my morning Bible study, I cradled my steaming cup of coffee and searched my heart. I felt God nudging me to buy another horse and to continue with the class. For two weeks I scoured western Montana and Wyoming until a friend of mine told me about a horse named Quincy. I was sure God had set him aside for me. The horse matched the description I'd written years ago in my dream book. I bought him, renamed him SkySong, and lined out a plan of how we could make up for the lost months of training.

The light breeze rustled SkySong's black mane as he nosed around in the dirt, looking for something to nibble. I put my hands on my hips. "There's hay in the feeder. Why don't you go eat that?" SkySong looked up at me with sad eyes and batted his long eyelashes. I shook my head.

Each day since I'd bought him I'd grown more disappointed. When I'd test ridden him, he'd seemed confident and bold, but it was almost as if I unloaded a different horse out of the trailer. I'd put him in his own metal paddock so he could adjust to his new surrounds without having to figure out the pecking order. But each time the metal gate squeaked open, SkySong quaked with fear and hunched in the corner. When I tried to slip the halter on, he'd snort and whirl away from me. *What happened to the confident horse I'd ridden a week ago?*

SkySong sauntered over to the wooden fence and leaned his head over, staring at the green grass. I rolled my eyes. "You're so timid I don't know if we'll ever catch up with our class." *Why did I ever think this was going to work? I wasted another chunk of money.*

SkySong switched his tail, looked over his shoulder at Dazzle and then at me. I shrugged my shoulders. "I'm not going to feed you separately forever. You've got to get this pecking order figured out." Closing the gate behind me, I shuffled to the house. My heart felt heavy. *Maybe it was silly to follow my dream. It'd be a whole lot less frustrating if I quit the class.*

The next morning Dazzle and SkySong hung their heads over the wooden rail and whinnied as I walked into their pasture to feed. When I tossed the hay into the feeder, Dazzle immediately dove in. SkySong walked to the other side and nibbled. Dazzle pinned her ears and barged around the feeder. SkySong reared up—right in her face and pawed the air with his front feet. Shocked, Dazzle retreated. I grinned and patted SkySong, "That a boy. Take a stand. Let her know you're serious."

But the next few mornings Dazzle put the run on him.

Saturday morning I pushed open the doors to the barn and grabbed flakes of hay. Dazzle and SkySong traipsed behind me. I tossed the hay into the rack and frowned as SkySong gingerly nibbled. Dazzle stood 10 feet behind him with her head hanging low. I stroked SkySong's neck. "What's up with her?" I strolled toward her. Dazzle stiffly lifted her head and hobbled toward me. A hump half the size of a basketball bulged from her black chest. Grimacing, I checked the injury and nervously laughed. "Well, girl, looks like you got it with both hind feet. Maybe you should have let him eat." SkySong had finally taken his stand, he'd had enough.

Deep inside me a question arose, *When are you going to take a stand for your dream?*

I gently twirled a strand of Dazzle's black mane as my mind wandered. Two weeks ago I was sure God had given me the horse of my dreams. *What had happened?* SkySong and I were making headway in the class. Sure, I wasn't as advanced as I wanted to be, but I was learning how to train a timid horse from the beginning—something I'd never done.

But I'd let the devil be at the top of the pecking order and bully me with the whip of discouragement. I'd been looking at the situation through eyes veiled with defeat instead of focusing on the wonderful opportunity God had given me. It wasn't time to quit. Instead it was time to rear up in the devil's face and kick his discouragement out. After all, SkySong and I still had four months of classes left.

*Lord, give me the courage to take a stand against the wiles of the devil. Amen.*

# 35

# The Zapper

*It is vain for you to rise up early, to sit up late,
to eat the bread of sorrows; for so
He gives His beloved sleep.*

PSALM 127:2 NKJV

Wispy golden and pink clouds floated across the summer evening sky as the sun slipped over the Rocky Mountain peaks. I heaved flakes of hay into the wooden feeder. Instantly Dazzle moved in and started munching. SkySong hesitantly walked up to the other side. He quickly grabbed stems of hay and then scampered a few feet away to chew them. I frowned and then grouched at him. "We went through this a few weeks ago. When will you quit being so jumpy about everything?"

I stood with my hands on my hips and watched SkySong move forward, nervously snatch more bites of hay, and then skitter 30 feet away to eat. I rolled my eyes. "I give up. When you get hungry, you'll belly up to the feeder."

It had been a long day at work, and I was exhausted. After taking care of the horses, I dragged myself into the house, pulled off my boots, and glanced at the clock. Ten fifteen. I felt like a zombie, I was so tired. By the time I read the mail, feed the cats, and played with my golden retriever puppy it was eleven thirty. After washing my face I tucked myself into bed and set the alarm for four o'clock.

Minutes after the alarm beeped I stood in the kitchen making coffee as I gulped down some granola. I was working a full-time job during the day and taking an intensive horse training class using SkySong. I was burning the candle at both ends. I had taken the time I needed for my schedule out of the only available spot—my sleep. *Lord, give me the energy to get through another day,* I prayed.

My tired body ached, I'd turned into a grump. I longed to go back to bed, but instead I hustled out to catch SkySong so I could train for an hour in the round pen before I zipped off to work. During my lunch hour I bought a hot dog at the Towne Pump gas station, snuck home, and trained a half hour. When I pulled into the driveway that evening, I could barely keep my eyes open. After changing into my barn clothes, I haltered up SkySong and trained him again.

In the fading sunlight I brushed SkySong and turned him loose in the corral. After throwing hay into the feeder, I stood by to watch. Dazzle calmly munched away, while SkySong timidly stole some stems and walked 10 feet away to chew them. I wagged my finger at him and admonished, "Get over it, SkySong. Just get in there and eat."

SkySong looked from side to side. He cautiously tiptoed to the feeder, strained his neck and stretched his lips to grab a few more wisps of hay. *Zap!* The bug zapper that hung over the feeder snapped and sizzled an enormous bug. SkySong wheeled on his haunches and raced to the other side of the corral. Wide-eyed, he turned and glared at the bug zapper. His neck arched, his nostrils flared.

I snickered. The big, black bug zapper had been there for years. It was just part of the landscape for Dazzle and me. When I'd first brought Sky-Song home, it was so cold outside that not many bugs had hatched so the zapper was mostly silent. But now that warm weather brought out the bugs, it snapped and popped all evening.

SkySong snorted and bobbed his head up and down. I looked at how scared he was, and then I felt bad. He had a reason to be jumpy. That bug zapper was pretty scary. Without warning it would zap and flash. After walking over to the zapper and unplugging the cord, I rubbed SkySong's neck. "I'm sorry, boy. That zapper can't get you now."

For the first time in days I didn't feel grumpy or irritated. Instead, compassion oozed out of me. I felt peaceful inside. I felt like me again.

*Why have I been so jumpy and grumpy?* I knew the culprit. Lack of sleep. *Why am I asking God for more energy so I can get through the long days? He's given me an incredible way to get refreshed—through sleep.*

I scratched SkySong's neck. "I won't be out first thing in the morning. I'm sleeping in until five thirty!"

In November SkySong and I celebrated our class graduation at the arena. The instructor stood next to SkySong and tipped his cowboy hat at me. He said, "You two have come a long way. I'm proud of what you've accomplished." My saddle creaked as I leaned forward and accepted the certificate from him. In spite of missing the first two months of classes, SkySong and I had worked through our frustrations and learned to communicate so well that we finished at the same level as the rest of the class.

*Lord, thank You for the gift of sleep so that my spirit, soul, and body can recharge. Amen.*

# 36

# Barbed Wire

*Jesus Christ never changes! He is the
same yesterday, today, and forever.*

HEBREWS 13:8 CEV

The aroma of spaghetti simmering in the crockpot made my stomach grumble. I could hardly wait until the guys came home from trucking the horses to the trailhead so we could eat. I leaned my left arm on the kitchen table, glanced at the checklist, and with a pencil scratched off "pack groceries for summer trip." Straightening up, I felt sticky from the sweltering August heat. I tucked a loose stand of long blond hair behind my ear. The phone jangled and I picked it up and said hello.

One of the crew, Rick, spoke, his voice tense. "Rebecca, you've got to come down to the pasture where the mares are. The new filly ran into the barbed wire. We're still hauling stock for the summer pack trip, so you need to take her to the vet."

I curled the phone cord around my finger. "It'll take me 15 minutes to get there. I'll need one of you to help me load the mare and the filly in the stock truck. For now, put them in the corral, make sure they have halters on, and put the ramp down on the truck so I can load and go." I hung up and then called the vet office to ask them to stand by. Grabbing the checkbook and the keys to the gold pickup, I headed out the door.

A cloud of dust kicked up behind me as I drove the dirt road to the pasture. Leaning my arm out the window, the breeze felt good. I grinned as I thought about the beautiful new filly that had been named Rahab. The boss had bought the mare two months ago while she was still in foal. She'd been bred late so the filly wasn't born until July. I frowned. *Why would Rahab run through barbed wire?* I slowed the truck to dodge a few potholes. *I hope this doesn't take too long. I've got to finish packing for the summer trip.* My mind nonchalantly drifted through the list of things I needed to get done tomorrow. The following day we'd be headed into the mountains on a 10-day trip. I wasn't prepared for what I'd see at the corrals or for what God was going to do.

Parking the truck next to the wooden corral, I hopped out. Waves of heat rose from the sandy soil. With his back to me, Rick stood in the corral, rolling up the sleeves of his blue plaid cowboy shirt. He held the mare's lead rope. The weathered corral gate stood ajar, and I slipped through. I could hear the filly suckling on the opposite side of the mare. "How's Rahab doing?"

Even though Rick's face was deeply tanned from a long summer working in the mountains, it looked white when he glanced up at me. My stomach flipped. *How bad is she?* I hustled around the mare and gasped. The bay filly looked like she'd been mauled by a bear. Her chest was slashed open from the outside of her right front shoulder all the way across her chest. The torn hide had fallen down and folded in a wrinkle at the top of her legs. Layers of muscle had been severed. The white bone of her dainty shoulder stuck out. Blood dripped down her legs. I gagged and turned my face away. Closing my eyes, I swallowed hard. "What happened?"

Rick kicked the toe of his leather boot in the sand, quickly glanced at me, and then looked away. "I've never seen anything like it. We were moving the mares at a walk into the next pasture, and all of a sudden this mare broke away from the herd with the filly on her heels. She headed straight for the barbed-wire fence. I cringed when I watched. The mare vaulted the fence and skidded to a stop. The filly hesitated.

The mare bellowed at her, calling her. The filly dug in her heels and sailed—squarely into the fence. The wires groaned but held. They sliced open her shoulder. The filly slid to the ground. The mare called her two more times, and each time the filly tried, the wire cut more of her shoulder. On the third try she popped between the wires to the other side." Rick shook his head. "It happened so fast there wasn't anything we could do."

Eyeing Rahab, I shuddered. "She's lost a lot of blood. Let's get them loaded. I hope she makes it to Missoula."

I positioned myself beside the filly with my arms looped under her belly to guide her. The mare followed Rick up the wooden ramp of the green stock truck, and the filly weakly wobbled behind her mom. A trail of blood stained the ramp. The filly leaned against the metal side tuckered out. We latched the doors and hoisted the ramp. I slid behind the wheel onto the hot vinyl seat. When I turned the key, the engine rumbled to life.

Gently I pulled onto the dirt road, not wanting to jar the mare and her babe. I rolled down the window and glanced at my watch: four fifty. *It'll take an hour to get to Missoula.* A cloud of dust rolled behind the truck. I tapped my fingers on the steering wheel. Dried blood was caked on my knuckles. *Is that filly strong enough to make it?* I reached down to turn on the radio. The engine slowed and sputtered. I glanced at the gauges and frowned. The gas gauge read "E". *Tank one is empty. The guys must have forgotten to fuel this morning before they started hauling stock.* I reached under the left side of the seat and flipped the switch that changed the truck over to the second fuel tank. My heart froze as I waited for the red needle to rise, my eyes glued to the gauge. The truck paused and then roared, but the needle still rested over "E". *Tank two is nearly empty too!*

My heart throbbed, and I glanced at my watch: four fifty-five. *It's seven miles to the gas station on the way to Missoula, but they close at five, and it's going to take me 15 minutes to get there.* I looked into the rearview mirror. A hole had been cut into the stock enclosure behind the driver's seat and covered with a metal grate so the driver could watch the horses. Rahab weakly leaned against the side of the truck. Blood still streamed down her front legs and pooled on the floor. My mind searched for options. *It's 12 miles to Ovando, and even if the gas station is closed, I can get Peggy or Howie to open the store for me. But it's the wrong direction...and that foal is bleeding to death.* The truck shook. Although the momentum kept it rolling forward, the engine died and I lost the power steering. *Tank two is empty.* I gripped the steering wheel with both hands. "God, You've got to help me! This filly is going to die if I get stuck out here."

The truck rolled forward. My knuckles were white. I swallowed hard. Suddenly the Bible story of when Jesus fed 5000 men with five loaves and two fish drifted through my thoughts. "Jesus, You multiplied the bread and the fish. I need You to multiply the gas so Rahab doesn't die." I took a deep breath. Reaching down, I flipped the switch back to the first tank and turned the ignition key. The needle read "E" but the truck shuddered, belched, and roared to life. My eyes darted to my watch: four fifty-seven. *Ovando is out of the question. I've got to head straight to the closest gas station.* "Lord, I need You to make sure that somebody works late at the gas station tonight."

Gravel crunched under the tires as the truck bounced down the dirt road. Finally I came to the stop sign on Highway 200. *Only a few more miles.* But when I accelerated up to speed, the truck's engine died. I gripped the steering wheel as the power steering went out again. Tank one was empty—again. The tires hummed on the asphalt. I gritted my teeth and then prayed, "Lord, give me gas—in Jesus' name!" I flipped the switch to tank two and turned the key. The truck bucked to life. Another mile marker flew past. And another. The truck sputtered and died just as I turned into the driveway of the red-and-white gas station. The power steering failed. I cranked on the steering wheel with all my might to maneuver the two-ton truck next to the pump. It rolled to a stop.

I glanced at the building just as the "Open" light in the window clicked off. I hopped out of the truck and ran for the door. A tall, wiry man walked out and locked it behind him.

"Sorry, we're closed. We should have been closed 15 minutes ago, but a motor home pulled in at the last minute, and it took him forever to fuel."

"But, mister, I've got to get fuel!"

His green eyes glared at me and then at the truck.

"I've got a filly in the back of my truck who is bleeding to death. I'm taking her to the vet." A tear dripped down my face as I pleaded, "And I'm out of gas in both tanks. I've got to have fuel!"

His eyes softened. "Well, why didn't you say so." He spun on his heels, rattled the lock open, and turned on the pump.

The veterinarian was waiting for me when I pulled the truck into the clinic's parking lot. We whisked Rahab inside and immediately prepped her for surgery. The doctor patched three separate layers of muscle groups before he sewed her hide together. Although Rahab had lost a good portion of her blood, she made it through surgery with flying colors.

Later that summer I had a chance to ask a mechanic about the gas tanks. Was it possible to have some gas that sloshed around in the tank after it officially ran out of gas? He shook his head. "The way those tanks are shaped, when that truck runs dry—it's dry."

I still marvel at that day. I witnessed three miracles! I'm convinced that God had the motor home stop and fuel up at the last minute so the station would be open for me. I'd driven a truck with two empty gas tanks. And Rahab lived.

*Lord, I'm so glad You're still in the miracle business! Amen.*

37

# The Gift

*Above all, clothe yourselves with love, which
binds us all together in perfect harmony.*

COLOSSIANS 3:14 NLT

The hot, dry August breeze rattled through the cottonwood leaves. A sorrel mare tied to one of the trees impatiently pawed as I doctored her filly. I dipped a sponge into a bucket of Betadine solution and wrung it out. Resting my left hand on the bay filly's withers, I squatted by her side. "Rahab, stand still so I can get you cleaned up." I gently wiped underneath the stiches that ran from the outside of her right front shoulder, across her chest, and to the point of her left shoulder. The wound had oozed lymph fluid and blood, which had crusted and dried on her velveteen fur. "We don't want this to draw flies and get infected."

The filly stiffened her neck. The curls of her short black mane danced in the breeze as she shook her head, as if telling me to hurry up.

I laughed. "Silly girl. I am hurrying." I swished the sponge in a separate bucket of water to rinse it. Just yesterday the filly had charged the barbed wire fence while she was trying to follow her mom, who had jumped the fence. The impact of her hitting the fence had slit her chest wide open. I shuddered as I remembered the moment I saw the delicate white bone of her shoulder exposed between bloody and mangled muscles. It was a miracle that she'd even lived.

The sun beat down on my back while I dipped the sponge in the antiseptic. The filly cocked her head side to side watching me. I swabbed the area around her stitches and worried. "I'm running out of time. What am I going to do with you tomorrow?"

I was going into the hills to cook on a 10-day summer pack trip, but Rahab needed to be doctored at least three times a day for the next two weeks. I groaned. Taking care of her would be time-consuming and demanding. She wasn't out of the woods yet. If she got a fever she could die within hours. *Who can take care of her?* My mind chugged through possibilities. *Maybe one of the guys who isn't going on the summer trip could doctor her?* I shook my head as I wiped caked blood from the filly's legs. A crew member had quit two weeks ago, and we were shorthanded. Worse yet, August was the month when we needed to get hunting camp set up. Over the next two weeks we'd be divided into two crews, both working in the hills. Nobody would be home to take care of Rahab. I tossed the sponge, and it landed in the rinse bucket with a splat. I shook my head. *That won't work.*

I reached into my shirt pocket and pulled out a foil-packed alcohol swab, a syringe, and a bottle of penicillin. *Maybe I'll stay out of the hills, and one of the guys on the summer crew can cook.* Ripping the alcohol packet open, I dug out the swab. Running my right hand down Rahab's back, I leaned over the top of her and wiped alcohol on the injection site on her buttocks. *Do any of them know how to do more than fry an egg? I doubt it.* I giggled. *I couldn't do that to the guests.*

After shaking the penicillin bottle, I stuck the needle through the rubber seal and drew back the plunger on the syringe. The penicillin was so thick and the needle so small that the liquid trickled into the syringe. *Maybe I should have one of crew stay out? Do any of them know how to give injections? Or would they know what to do if the wound got infected?* I pulled the needle out of the bottle and flicked the syringe with my index finger to knock the air to the top. Making a fist, I bopped the filly's butt a couple times to numb the injection site and then stuck the needle in. I froze as Rahab stepped forward.

She turned her head and batted her long black eyelashes at me. Slowly I pushed the plunger.

After turning Rahab and her mom loose, I gathered the first aid supplies in my arms and headed to the house. My mind whirled as I put the penicillin in the refrigerator and tucked the rest away. *What am I going to do? I can't just leave her.* Frustrated, I grabbed the keys to the pickup and slipped on my sunglasses. The truck needed fuel before I headed to the trailhead.

I pulled up by the gas pump of the Ovando Mercantile and hopped out of the truck. The hot breeze swirled dust across the road. My friend Peggy stood pumping gas on the other side of the island. I nodded and pushed the sunglasses on top of my head. "Hi, Peggy," I said as I slipped the nozzle into the gas tank and clicked it on.

She smiled, tucking a brown strand of hair behind her ear. "How's that filly doing this morning?"

"She's perky for having her chest torn up so bad." I frowned. "But I don't know what to do with her when I go into the hills tomorrow. I was trying to figure out which one of the crew could cook so I could stay out." I chuckled. "But then I figured if I wanted the guests to come back, I'd better ditch that idea."

Peggy laughed and said, "That's easy. Bring her over. Howie, the girls, and I will take care of her."

I felt like kicking myself. *Why did I say anything? She's got more than enough to do at her ranch without taking care of the mare and my wounded filly.* I shook my head and scuffed my boot in the gravel. "Thanks, but that's too much. I'll get it figured out."

A glint passed through Peggy's eyes, as if she were hurt.

Peggy and I small-talked about the local happenings. She hung up the gas nozzle and went inside to pay. A few minutes later I traipsed up the weathered wooden stairs just as a white-haired gentleman with his arms full of groceries was struggling through the door. I skipped a step and reached for it, saying, "Can I help you with that?"

He shifted one of the bags onto his hip and gruffed at me, "I've got it."

His words stung. I stepped to the side and huffed to myself, *Thank you too! I was just trying to help.* Slipping inside, I winced. *Isn't that what I just did to Peggy?* Her offer to take care of Rahab was a gift of love. She had plenty of experience doctoring animals and knew the time commitment involved in taking care of the mare and filly. She wanted to help, and I desperately needed her. *Why didn't I accept?* I chewed on my lip. *Was it because I don't want to be a burden? Or because I want to be the one doing the giving? Why? Receiving makes me feel vulnerable.*

An odd thought crossed my mind. *Her gift was like a kiss from God, but I turned my cheek.* I'd never viewed it that way. Love is like giving a beautifully wrapped package. The sparkling package could sit on the shelf collecting dust for decades but it wouldn't do any good. The person needed to receive it and open it. Love needed a receiver as much as a giver to be complete.

The cowbells that hung on the door jangled as a rancher stepped in, bringing me back to reality. I looked up as Peggy walked through the grocery aisle toward me. I took a deep breath and asked, "Peggy, were you serious about wanting to doctor that filly?"

Peggy nodded. "You know I was."

I stumbled over my words. "I—I sure could use the help. I—I don't know what else to do."

Peggy pulled her truck keys out of her jeans pocket. "I'm headed home now. Why don't you bring them over?"

And it worked out great. Rahab thrived at Peg and Howie's. There wasn't anybody who could have provided better care than they did. Through Rahab's recovery, I discovered that oftentimes God meets my needs through gifts of love from my friends. It was time to quit turning my cheek.

*Lord, please help me graciously receive from my friends and show me how I can return gifts of love. Amen.*

38

## Aliens!

*The LORD watches over the strangers.*

PSALM 146:9 NKJV

Beads of sweat rolled behind Czar's ears. My body swayed in the saddle with the rhythm of his footsteps. A long line of guests on horseback drifted behind me. This was one of my favorite rides. The trail meandered through meadows blooming with wildflowers, wound through corridors of tall pines, and skirted grassy hillsides. Now the trail narrowed and clung to rocky ledges over Basin Creek, which chortled below. Oftentimes the deep, blue pools had enormous fish. I leaned over the water and grinned as I dreamed of casting a fishing lure into the creek and trolling from horseback.

I leaned forward and stroked my bay's sweaty neck. "We're almost to where we'll camp tonight." I sighed because it felt so good to be back in the hills with my life moving at three miles per hour—the speed of my horse. I'd been in civilization almost two weeks between summer pack trips, and that was two weeks too long for me. Today was the fifth day of a weeklong trip. It'd taken me until yesterday to decompress from the phones, newspapers, TV, radio, and hustle and bustle of everyday living. The solitude of the wilderness was seeping into my soul. *Well almost.* I bristled. *It would if Ron and Sue would go to sleep instead of talking into the wee hours of the morning. Why do they have to pitch their tent right next to mine?*

Every afternoon when we pulled off the trail and tied up the horses, Sue would wander over to me. As I unloaded the packs from the mules, she would nonchalantly ask, "Where do you think you'll pitch your tent?" The first day I thought, *That's nice, she's asking so she doesn't put their tent where I want to be.* But that wasn't the case. Instead, they pitched their tent almost on top of the spot I'd chosen. I wondered, *Perhaps they misunderstood me?* But the next night they did the same thing. I wouldn't have minded if they would have crawled into their sleeping bags and fell right to sleep. But instead they were like little kids who kept themselves awake. They talked about the ride that day, the flowers they'd seen, and everything else under the sun. I felt like I was at a high school bunking party. Last night I even pulled my brown sleeping bag over my head, trying to drown out their voices. But it didn't work. *We're out in the middle of the wilderness. Why can't they give me some space?*

I reined Czar down the small hill. Hooves clattered over the pebbles that lined the creek. We splashed in, and the water current buffeted every step until Czar scrambled on shore. One by one the horses heaved up the grassy bank, stopped, and shook. We wandered through the trees along the creek until we came to a small meadow. The guests and I dismounted and tied the horses to the rope corral already set up. I grinned as I flopped the stirrup over the top of my saddle and loosened the cinch. *I know exactly what I'm going to say this time.*

After all the guests had stacked their riding saddles on the canvas tarp, we waded through the tall grass toward the string of mules tied under a lone pine tree where we would set up our kitchen tarp. The wranglers had unloaded most of them. I walked over to the pile of packs that contained our duffels and loosened the rope on a load. While I unwrapped the canvas, Sue sauntered over.

"Any tents?"

I nodded, pulled out a green bundle, and handed it to her.

"There are so many great spots to pitch a tent," she said. "Have you thought about where you're going to put yours?"

Winding up the mantie rope, I pointed to my left at a cluster of pines. "There are some flat grassy spots by those trees. And there are some more nice ones over there." I pointed to my right. "I haven't decided yet." The next half hour I watched Ron and Sue out of the corner of my eye as the wranglers and I set up camp. They walked back and forth, stalling. Instead of pitching my tent before dinner, I decided to wait. The coffee simmered and the smoke from the wood-stove formed a ribbon all the way across the valley before Ron and Sue finally walked over to the small grove of pines. I heard the clatter of the aluminum tent poles as they dumped the tent out of its stuff sack. After washing dishes, I grabbed a tent and my sleeping bag, and then I walked at right angles to Ron and Sue. I didn't want to be rude, but I was going to be out of earshot. Once I snuggled down into my sleeping bag, it only took minutes to fall asleep.

The next day Ron and Sue followed me like puppy dogs. They rode directly behind me along the trail and sat next to me at lunch. By midafternoon I was wondering what I was going to say about the tent. It was obvious they were glued to me and weren't going to let me out of their sight. *What is wrong with them?* I wondered. *I'm going to need a surgeon to separate us when we get to the trailhead.*

Cotton-ball clouds drifted overhead, casting shadows across the mountainside. The long line of horses and mules carefully placed their feet between the rocks on the trail. Breathing heavily, they labored uphill for several miles. We topped the hill into the boulder-strewn grassy bowl of Hahn Pass. I noticed a few backpackers on the trail about 100 yards ahead. Turning in my saddle, I yelled, "Backpackers!"

Sue, who rode behind me, turned around and passed the word. Each guest in the long line echoed the message. Sue yelled up to me, "Rebecca, why does it matter that there are backpackers ahead?"

I scooted my weight to the left side of my saddle and turned sideways. "It does. The horses and mules don't care for them."

Sue lifted her shoulders and commented, "That's strange."

"Not really. When you work with horses and mules, you need to get inside their heads and figure out what they're thinking. If you can look at the world through their eyes, it makes them a lot easier to understand." Czar dropped his head to snatch a bite of green grass. I tapped my heels to his side to make him pick up his head and walk faster. "I think they're scared because the pack frames hang above the person's head, like antennas." I giggled. "I've often wondered if the critters think that the backpacks are part of the person's body—like they're deformed aliens."

Sue raised her eyebrows. "So they're afraid of them?"

Nodding, I chuckled. "Sometimes they get so freaked out that they snort and blow or jump sideways."

Sue's knuckles turned white as she gripped the reins.

My eyebrows creased when I noticed Sue's fear. In my mind, I found it amusing that the horses looked at backpackers as if they were aliens. That understanding gave me the ability to help them overcome their fears. But Sue wasn't amused. Fear etched lines across her face. Deep in thought, with my right hand I slapped the ends of my reins against my chaps. My mind replayed my words. *You need to get inside their heads and figure out what they're thinking…look at the world through their eyes.*

I hadn't tried to "get into" Ron and Sue's heads. I glanced back at her. Sue's face was as white as a ghost. *Can that be why they camp next to my tent? And why they talk all night like little kids who don't want to go to sleep? Kids don't go to sleep when they're afraid.* Suddenly it was obvious. Ron and Sue were from the city. They'd never been in the wilderness. They were afraid of everything around them because it was unfamiliar. I took a deep breath. *They were really courageous to come into the wilderness.* And I hadn't done anything to help them overcome their fear. *Perhaps if I start explaining things to her, she'll understand and it'll dissolve her fears.*

I twisted sideways. "Sue, I'm going to swing off the trail, and I want you to follow me. We'll take a wide berth around the backpackers. By doing that, the horses and mules won't feel threatened and they'll walk past calmly."

Sue nodded and relaxed into her saddle.

I reined Czar into the knee-deep grass. The long line of guests followed. We waved at the group of backpackers and shouted greetings. The horses and mules eyed them, but stayed calm.

Guiding Czar onto the trail, another thought drifted through my mind. *I wonder what God thought about me brushing Ron and Sue and their fears aside?* My heart sank. *They're strangers here. They're my guests.* The next couple miles I chewed on the idea of how I could help them. When we pulled into our next camp area on Monture Creek, I slowed Czar and motioned for Sue to ride alongside. I pointed to my left at a large flat spot under some tall pines. "I'm going to pitch my tent over there. There's plenty of room for yours too."

Sue smiled.

Before that trip I'd never thought about adults being afraid of my everyday world. I discovered that often when I don't understand people, it's because they are acting out of fear. But when I look at the situation through their eyes and also through God's, God helps me understand them.

*Lord, when I don't understand those around me, please remind me to "get inside" their heads and look at life from their perspective. Amen.*

# 39

# The Elephant Box

*I wisdom dwell with prudence, and find
out knowledge of witty inventions.*

Proverbs 8:12 KJV

The truck keys jangled as I pulled them off the hook by the back door. I reached for the doorknob, and Cochise, my black-and-silver German shepherd, whimpered from his pile of blankets on the kitchen floor. His toenails scratched the floor. He cried as he dragged himself toward me. Quickly I turned and commanded, "No." He stopped and looked up at me, his brown eyes pleading. I crouched by his side and caressed his head. "You have to stay here, buddy." I grimaced as I looked at his battered and skinned-up face. A zigzag row of stiches lined his shaved chest. I gently rubbed his ear. "I'll be back in a bit."

The day before yesterday Cochise had wandered up onto Highway 200, and a car had crashed into him, throwing him over the roof of the car. It was a miracle that he lived and didn't break any bones. He was black-and-blue from his ears to his paws and had lumps from swellings in several places on his body. He'd lost a lot of hide from "road rash" and had to be sutured in several places. He couldn't walk on his own, so when he needed to go outside he'd whine for me. I'd scoop up his 85-pound body and shuffle out the door to the grass where I'd loop my arms under his chest to balance him. I was grateful he was alive.

I slid behind the steering wheel of the Ford pickup and rolled down the window to let out the August heat. I sighed. *What am I going to do with Cochise when I go to the hills?* He was still in critical condition and needed a lot of care. Tomorrow all the crew, including me, was headed down the trail, either on a two-week summer pack trip or a work trip. I knew that none of my ranch friends would be able to take care of him because it was haying season. They'd be busy in the fields. My outfitter friends would be in the mountains.

The truck chugged up the hill into the small ranch community of Ovando. A large American flag waved in the afternoon breeze above the quaint cinderblock building containing the post office. I tapped my fingers on the steering wheel as I reviewed my options. *I could drive down to the veterinary clinic in Missoula and leave him there, but the vet said it might take a month before he could run the trails again. That'd be horribly expensive.* Besides, he's a typical German shepherd, totally devoted to his owner—me. I was concerned if I left him someplace he might believe I'd abandoned him and lose his will to live. I chewed on my lip. The year before last, my German shepherd Kai had gotten killed. Last year my saddle horse broke her leg and had to be put down. Emotionally I couldn't handle losing another animal. "God, what am I going to do? I'm plumb out of ideas. But if You have one, would You please let me know?"

I parked the truck in front of the post office and hopped out. After digging a stack of mail out of my post office box, I walked over to the counter and sorted it. I'd gotten some magazines I knew I wouldn't have time to read. Walking over to set them on the table in the corner so somebody else could enjoy them, my eye caught the cover of a magazine. It had a photograph of an elephant with a coach style box on top of him with a person riding inside. Something tweaked my spirit. *That's a crazy idea!* I blinked and stared. *That wouldn't work.* I picked up the magazine. *Or could it? God, is this it?* My heart raced. *Could I do that for Cochise? Is there a way I could rig a box to go on top of one of the mule's pack saddles? That way he could go with me, and I could take care of him.*

Dust swirled up behind the pickup as I raced down the gravel road to the end-of-the-road camp. The guys on crew were tossing hay into the hay bunks for the horses and mules when I pulled in. I excitedly told them my crazy idea and asked, "What do you think?" They nodded their heads and laughed as they strolled to the corral to catch Tag, a tall, rawboned and gangly black mule—and probably the only mule in the outfit that would let a dog ride on his back.

While they brushed and saddled him, I ducked into the tack trailer to look for the perfect wooden kitchen box. A large, blue, rectangular one caught my eye. It was the perfect size: 2-feet wide by 3-feet long by 16-inches deep. Grabbing a screwdriver, I took the hinged lid off, making it an open-topped box. *The sides will cradle Cochise,* I thought.

I lugged the box out the door as the guys finished slinging packs on both sides of Tag. I grinned. "Great idea! We can toss the box on top. It'll perch in the middle. The packs will support the box from underneath and keep it from sliding off."

Bob tipped his brown cowboy hat and grinned. He lifted the box out of my hands and heaved it on top of Tag. Tag groaned his usual deep moan as Bob tied the box on top with ropes. Tag never failed to groan, no matter how heavy or how light the load was. Untying the lead rope, Bob led Tag through camp. I jumped up and down and clapped my hands as the box swayed side to side but rode steady. "Yes...yes...yes!"

The next morning the sun filtered shafts of light through the pines as we finished loading all the mules. A cool, summer breeze gently rustled the tall grass. The guys had roped the elephant box onto Tag's packsaddle, and I had stuffed it with blankets. We were ready to hit the trail except for loading Cochise. I scooped him off the passenger seat of the pickup. "Okay, buddy, you're going for a ride." With his head hanging over my left arm and my right arm looped under his rear, I lugged him over to Tag.

Bob stood waiting and gently gathered Cochise's rear in his arms.

I glanced at Tag and watched for any objections. "Tag, are you ready?" Tag swiveled his long black ears and listened, but he stood relaxed. I looked Bob in the eye. "One…two…three…heave." We swung Cochise over the side of the box and slowly lowered him inside.

Tag groaned. He twisted his head around and stared at Cochise as if asking, "What are you doing?"

I laughed.

Cochise whined as he rustled into a comfortable position. Settling in, he rested his chin on the corner. I scratched his ears. "No getting out," I ordered. I glanced at Bob. "Do you think you could lead Tag a lap or two?" Bob untied the lead rope and led Tag around camp. The box swayed with every step, and I walked alongside. Tag's long black ears were tuned in on Cochise and me. At first Cochise whimpered and his eyes grew wide. I patted his head and cooed, "See, you get to come on the trip with us. Isn't this fun?" Cochise looked deep into my eyes and relaxed.

Bob stopped near Czar and said, "Mount up. I'll hand you Tag's lead rope."

I untied Czar from the hitching rail and swung my leg over the saddle. Reining Czar next to Bob I took the lead rope. Cochise propped his chin on the edge of the box again. I turned out the gate with Tag lumbering behind, followed by the guests, and then the pack strings.

Cochise enjoyed his ride. Tag made the perfect "elephant" and enjoyed the extra attention. Over the next week, every time we passed another group on the trail they laughed and pointed at the elephant box with the dog peeking over the edge. They all commented, "I've never seen anything like it." I wasn't surprised; I hadn't either.

When the second week rolled around, Cochise walked part of the day. By the end of the trip he rarely rode in the box. Within a month he raced down the trail like he'd never been hurt.

I've never forgotten the elephant box. I believed that God cared enough about a wounded dog and his master that He showed me that witty idea. I've often wondered, *Did God have an angel put that magazine on the top of the stack at the post office?*

> *Lord, help me to be open-minded to Your solutions. Give me the courage to follow them—even if they sound crazy. Amen.*

40

# Venison Jerky

*Let them do good, that they be rich in good
works, ready to give, willing to share.*

1 TIMOTHY 6:18 NKJV

Hoofbeats of 18 head of horses and mules drummed on the hard-packed, dirt trail. My body swayed in the saddle with the rhythm of Czar's steps. The sun beat down on my shoulders, and the air was still. It was going to be another sweltering day. Rye, my black German shepherd trotted in front of me, panting. A squirrel that sat on a dead log switched its tail and chattered at her. Rye's ears perked, and she raced headlong toward it. The squirrel clambered up a pine tree, moved onto a branch, and scolded her. Rye whined and clawed at the trunk. I smiled. "You never tire of that game, do you?"

Today was a moving day on a summer pack trip. Bill, the boss, had ridden ahead with the guests. Brett and Darrin, both wranglers, each led a string of mules. While the guests and Bill stopped to eat lunch, Brett, Darrin, and I would ride past, eating lunch in the saddle. Later in the afternoon we would pull into the next meadow where we were going to camp and get everything set up before Bill and the guests rode in. I enjoyed riding the trails with just the wranglers and the pack strings. It gave me hours of quiet time to think and pray.

My mind drifted to last Sunday. On my day off I'd sat in church and listened to an evangelist excitedly share about his mission trip to Africa. As he spoke, my heart longed to do something for God that impacted people's lives in a big way. My tummy grumbled. I unbuckled my saddlebags and pulled out a Ziploc bag of jerky. I turned and yelled, "I brought some of my homemade venison jerky. Do either of you want a piece for lunch?"

In sync they both yelled back, "Sure!"

Reining Czar to the side of the trail, I waited for Darrin to ride alongside. A long line of mules trudged behind him, their loads rocking side to side. Methodically they marched on. With each step, a cloud of dust swirled from their feet. It hung in the air so thickly that I could barely see Brett, who rode behind Darrin's last mule.

I handed a piece of jerky to Darrin. He reached with his left hand at the same time his lead mule pulled back, yanking him backward. The jerky fell to the ground. Instantly Rye snatched it.

Darrin grimaced as he rode past. I nudged Czar forward. "I'll get you another." Czar trotted while I juggled the reins and dug out another piece. A low-hanging pine bough slapped me in the face and threatened to steal my cowboy hat. Slapping a hand to my head, I pushed the hat down tight and reined Czar away from the row of pines. When Czar was next to Darrin's horse again, I leaned out of the saddle. This time Darrin grabbed the jerky.

"This is great. Thanks."

I reined Czar further off the trail. Darrin's mules plodded past with their long ears flopping. As Brett's horse trudged closer, I lined up Czar and kicked him into a walk. A cloud of dust enveloped us as we both stretched out of the saddles. Brett grabbed the jerky. The trail narrowed. In a few feet it skirted a hillside. There wasn't any way I could ride to the front, so I waited while Brett's string rolled past. When I pulled in behind Brett's last mule, I heard him yell, "Thanks!"

Coughing from all the dust, I choked, "You're welcome." As soon as the trail widened, I wanted out of the dust bowl. I turned Czar into the trees, kicked him into a trot, and swung wide so I could get back to the front. I ducked pine boughs as Czar trotted over downed logs and swerved around trees until we passed Darrin. Sticking a piece of jerky into my mouth, I pulled onto the trail. *All that for a couple pieces of jerky,* I thought.

Sweat dripped down Czar's deep-red neck as the afternoon wore on. Off and on I prayed for friends, family, and the evangelist. My tummy grumbled. I thought about eating a piece of jerky, but I didn't want to eat it in front of Darrin. *And if I offer one to him, I need to offer one to Brett too. I enjoy sharing, but do I really want to go through all that hassle again? Too bad I don't have a super long stick…like a big set of tongs.* I smiled as I imagined tongs long enough to hand Brett a piece.

My tummy rumbled again. My saddle groaned as I turned and hollered, "Do you guys want another piece of jerky?"

They both chimed, "Yes."

Digging into my saddlebags, I reined Czar to the side of the trail. *Whop!* A pine bough slapped my chest. Quickly I brushed it aside. My eyes grew wide. *I don't need tongs. The solution was here all along. It was whacking me in the face. I needed to use what I had at hand.*

Gathering the reins, I kicked Czar into a fast walk and scanned the trail. Ahead a pine bough stuck over the trail like a hand. It was about shoulder high. I nudged Czar toward it and held the jerky over my head. "Hey, Darrin, here's your jerky!" I called. Waving my hand, I set it on the pine needles as I rode past. I swiveled around to watch.

Darrin laughed as he picked up his jerky.

Chuckling, I searched for another bough. Riding to the other side of the trail I held a piece of jerky over my head and yelled, "Brett, here's yours!" I felt smug as I turned and watched Brett retrieve it.

Miles down the trail my thoughts wandered back to the evangelist's trip to Africa. *God, someday I'd really like to do something for You that makes a big difference in people's lives.*

A squirrel sat on a pine bough and squawked at Rye as she trotted past. While I watched the squirrel's tail flick and the branch wave, a thought bubbled out of my spirit: *You are. You're using what you have at hand.* I pondered the words. Just like passing the jerky, I'd made it complicated to do things for God. I didn't have to go to Africa to impact people's lives. I could sit right here in my saddle and pray. I grinned. *And I can share what I have with others.* I leaned back. I *was* making a difference—one prayer and one piece of jerky at a time.

> *Lord, open my eyes to the opportunities that are in front of me and that will impact people for You. Amen.*

# 41

## *Trash*

*You yourself must be an example to them by doing
good works of every kind. Let everything you do
reflect the integrity and seriousness of your teaching.*

Titus 2:7 NLT

White, billowy clouds drifted over Center Ridge and across the
deep-blue sky. The tops of the lodgepole pine trees swayed in
the afternoon breeze. Czar's hooves clopped on the dusty trail as he
slowly trotted toward Monture Camp. His deep-red coat glistened as
his muscles flexed. His black mane gently swirled with each step. I
sat deep in the saddle, breathing in the crisp smell of the pines. It felt
so good to relax and have the trail to myself. I was riding into camp
ahead of the summer guests so I could have a hot dinner ready when
they rode in. This was my time to unwind. The last few days had been
hectic. I'd finished a summer pack trip two days ago and had a to-do
list a mile long to get ready for this trip. *I hope I remembered everything.*

A flash of movement deep within a stand of pines caught my eye. I
glanced around the trunk of a tree. A deer stood stone still, although
her ears followed us as we drifted past. Out of habit I glanced at the
trail to see if there were any fresh tracks. The dust held deep imprints
from several horses and mules. *Oh no. I forgot to call Karrie and get
the dates of their hunts.* Jim and Karrie ran an outfitting business and

rode past Monture Camp on the way to their camp. I liked to mark their hunting dates on my calendar so I could bake treats for them. These were probably their tracks. *I can't believe it. I told her I'd call.* I slouched in my saddle. *I'll have to do it after this trip.*

Miles floated past. Droplets of sweat formed behind Czar's ears, and I slowed him to a walk. The hot breeze carried the smell of rain. I glanced up. Dark clouds formed a line and marched across the sky. It looked like we'd be in for a late-afternoon thundershower. I grimaced. *And I told Caroline that I'd write out a list of things I needed her to pick up in town—and we need another nylon tarp for end-of-the-road.*

The trail wound around the mountain, crossed a creek, and then climbed up onto a flat bench. At the top of the hill something yellow caught my eye. I squinted. It was about the size of a grapefruit—but it wasn't one. I half stood in my stirrups. *What can it be?*

It skittered and rolled. Czar cocked his head and stared at it. I gathered the reins in case he jumped. He walked several more steps and I chuckled. It was an empty margarine container. *But what is it doing next to the trail?*

Reining in Czar, I stepped out of the saddle and picked it up. The container had punctures in it from fangs—bear fangs. Bear tracks criss-crossed the trail. *Why is a bear packing a margarine container down the trail?* Puzzled, I stuffed it into my saddlebags and mounted up.

I nudged Czar into a walk. The trail opened into a corridor between the lodgepole pines. A half mile later, it forked, one side leading to Monture Camp. Czar stretched his legs, knowing that as soon as we got into camp he'd get a pan of grain. In a few steps I spotted another yellow margarine container...and another. The whole bench was dotted with trash. Empty milk boxes and instant oatmeal packages had been chewed and strewn. It looked like a couple of bears had had a party. And I knew where they'd gotten all of it—out of my cook tent! I scooped up the trash, stuffed it into my saddlebags, and kicked Czar into a lope up the trail and into camp.

Tying Czar to the hitching rail, I ran for the cook tent. Empty containers littered the floor. *Trashy bears! How dare they leave a mess behind that I have to clean up!* I squatted to pick up an empty oatmeal box. I noticed a hole in the knee of my jeans. *Oh no. I'd told the guys that I'd mend their jeans for them—and I'd totally spaced it.* I rubbed my forehead. *What was I thinking?* I had great intentions, and I'd made all kinds of promises. But the promises were empty just like these containers. I'd strewn them around carelessly, not unlike the trash the bears had left behind. Good intentions didn't mean a thing without action backing them up.

Tossing away the empty containers, I determined in my heart that from now on I wasn't going to talk about good intentions or make promises. Instead I was simply going to do—and let my actions speak for themselves.

*Lord, teach me how to be a person of action instead of just words so I'm a good example of You. Amen.*

42

## The Lid

*Your faith should not be in the wisdom
of men but in the power of God.*

1 Corinthians 2:5 nkjv

The morning sunlight danced through the forest, and the cool breeze whispered through the lodgepole pines. From a branch overhead, a squirrel scolded. My bay gelding, Czar, stood saddled and napping at the hitching rail outside of Carmichael Cabin. Next to him, Little Girl, my brown mule, slowly switched her tail. I sat on the wooden cabin step by the one-burner propane stove, on which a blue, enamelware coffeepot belched steam. I lifted the pot off the stove and poured boiling water through the funnel-shaped coffee maker into my white-plastic "go cup." My mouth watered as the aroma floated on the breeze. This was my morning luxury—one cup of coffee while I rode down the trail. Luxuries in my life were few and far between while I worked for the US Forest Service as a wilderness ranger.

For 10 days at a time I disappeared into the Bob Marshall Wilderness Complex to do wilderness studies. I worked alone, riding Czar and leading Little Girl. My black German shepherd, Rye, faithfully trotted by my side. Because I only had one pack animal to carry all my clothes, winter jacket, dishes, pots and pans, food, tent, sleeping bag, axe, saw, first aid kit, and so forth for 10 days, there wasn't room for the comforts of life. But I always had a big stash of freshly ground coffee. I delighted in making each cup individually—and strong enough to float a horseshoe.

I watched the last of the water drip through the filter, filling the cup. *Umm, black gold.* Shutting off the propane burner, I tucked it inside the cabin door and padlocked the door. Picking up the go-cup, I walked toward the Czar. Coffee sloshed out of the cup and dribbled down my jeans. *Oh, I wish I hadn't lost the lid.*

Yesterday was the first day of a 10-day hitch. I'd ridden 18 miles into the wilderness. Like every other morning, I'd jumped into the saddle sipping coffee. After I downed the last drop, I buckled the cup to the outside of my saddlebag. At lunch I'd used the cup to dip water out of the North Fork of the Blackfoot River. Somewhere along the next stretch of trail the lid had popped off. When I unsaddled Czar last night I discovered it was missing. I'd shrugged it off thinking, *It shouldn't be too hard to find.* Each day I'd be riding portions of the same trail, and much of the area had been burned last year. The lid was fire-engine red. *The bright red against charred black should be easy to see.*

When I got to the hitching rail, Czar lazily opened his eyes. I rubbed the small white star on his forehead. "Time to go to work." Untying Czar's lead rope, I set the steaming cup on top of the hitching rail. I untied Little Girl. Holding her lead, I swung into the saddle on Czar. The saddle squeaked as I settled in and nudged him forward. I planned on circling the hitching rail close enough to reach over and pick up the cup. But as Little Girl walked past, she switched her tail, knocking the cup off the rail. The steaming coffee spilled across the ground. "Doggone, Little Girl! What did you do that for?" Pouting, I slipped out of the saddle, scooped up the cup, and buckled it onto my saddlebag. "I've got to find that lid."

Every step along the trail I searched. I even watched where Rye snuffled along the trail, thinking she'd find it. Nothing. That night while sitting on the cabin's porch and heating a can of chili, the thought of the lid bugged me. *It's just a lid, Rebecca. What's the big deal?* But it continued to haunt me. Partly because it was a piece of equipment I'd lost. And keeping track of my equipment in the backcountry was an extremely important habit that I'd ingrained into myself. But also because the lid made it possible to savor my coffee each morning.

Every day as I rode the trail, I hunted for that fire-engine-red lid. First I focused on watching the left side of the trail. Then the right. I slipped out of the saddle and walked, hoping that I'd see it from a lower point of view. I scolded myself for losing it. And then I did the same for bothering to search for it. But I continued to rattle bushes and peer over cliffs. Nothing.

The last day of my hitch I sat on the cabin porch finishing my last bite of granola. Czar and Little Girl dozed at the hitching rail. The morning sun cast rays from behind a mountain peak. The birds chirped their morning songs. Rye spotted a squirrel and chased him up a lodge-pole pine. He sat on a branch and scolded her. I poured boiling water through my filter. *Where can that lid be? I've searched everywhere imaginable.* I rubbed my hands on my black jeans. *God, this sounds silly. You've got so many bigger things to do. There are people out there with real needs.* I sighed and looked at the clouds that slowly floated like cotton balls across the crystalline-blue sky. *I feel stupid asking, but You see all things. You know where it is. Will You show me?*

Hustling around the cabin, I gathered my gear and loaded the packs on Little Girl. I swung into the saddle and reined Czar onto the trail. Rye trotted in front of us, snuffling and exploring. The trail wound through a stand of pines, across a grassy side hill, and onto a flat. We rode into the burned forest. What had been pine trees were now charred spears poking out of the ground. Their blackened branches were bare. Hoofbeats drummed on the dirt trail as I turned and glanced around. Not a green needle in sight. The fire had burned so hot in this area that it had sterilized the ground. Now, a year later, nothing had grown above the thick layer of ash that carpeted the forest floor.

Suddenly Rye stopped. She stared. Her ears pointed forward. Crouching, she wiggled her rear and gathered her hind legs underneath her. She pounced. A squirrel raced toward the nearest tree with Rye hot on its tail. The squirrel leaped for the trunk and clawed its way up the bark. Rye jumped up the tree, coming up short. The squirrel scolded as it ran to the notch in the tree where it had rebuilt its nest after the fire. I eyed the nest. Charred sticks lay in a heap on the branch…and something bright red was…I squinted. "My lid!" I laughed. I'd ridden this section of trail every day, and I had looked everywhere except up. I shook my head. I hadn't found it until I looked up—up to God to ask for His wisdom and guidance.

It wasn't about the lid being too small for Him to get involved. It was about my being willing to ask for His wisdom and power to manifest in *every* area of my life. *If I'm not asking God about the lid, what else am I not asking Him about?*

Slipping out of the saddle, I rummaged through the ash on the ground until I uncovered a long stick. I climbed back into the saddle with the stick in my left hand. I positioned Czar directly under the nest. The squirrel chattered as he watched me. I patted Czar's neck. "Stand still, okay?" I knelt on the saddle. Gathering my feet underneath me, I slowly stood. I lifted the stick and poked the lid. It fell onto the trail. I shouted "Yes!" and slid back into the saddle. Rye grabbed the lid and playfully tossed it into the air.

While working alone the rest of the summer, there were lots of opportunities for me to rely on my own understanding. But then that fire-engine-red lid would come to mind. So, instead, I practiced sharing with God about everything, great and small. Then I'd be quiet and listen to the One who is the wisest of all.

*Lord, help me be willing to ask for Your wisdom in every area of my life—even in trivial matters. Amen.*

# 43

# Shear Wind

*But you, LORD, are a shield around me, my*
*glory, the One who lifts my head high.*

PSALM 3:3

Birds flitted past, playing on the light breeze that carried the rancid stench of aging charcoal. I narrowed my nostrils and breathed shallow breaths. It smelled acidic and putrid. A raven's caw echoed through the eerie remains. Skeletal, charred pines studded the mountains as far as I could see. Several of the dead trees precariously leaned against each other. Others lay in piles 20 to 30 trees deep, stacked like pick-up sticks.

Last year a wild fire had burned more than 240,000 acres of this forest, and I was riding through one of the hot spots. The forest fire had burned so intensely here that not even the grass had grown back. Instead, everything was blackened with soot that soaked up and then radiated the heat from the sun. I felt like I was riding inside an oven with its temperature set on broil. Little did I know that in a few minutes the heat would disappear, and I would discover how deadly the remains of this forest could become.

Squirrels chittered and chased each other along the dead branches. Hooves drummed on the hard-packed dirt trail that wound down the fold of the mountain. Czar plodded along. I slouched in the saddle, lulled by the August sun that scorched against my cotton shirt. Pulling my red bandana out of my pocket, I wiped the sweat off the back of my neck. A thin film of gray trail dust stained the cloth. *It's going to feel so good to take a hot shower tonight.* Today was the last day of a 10-day ride for the US Forest Service.

Tipping down the brim of my black cowboy hat to block the sun's glare, I turned and glanced behind me at the loads on Little Girl, my brown pack mule. Her packs rocked evenly. With every step, a puff of dirt and ash rose from the trail and hung in the air. Behind her my black German shepherd, Rye, trotted with her head hung low, panting. In a few steps Czar picked up his pace. He knew the horse trailer was parked at the end-of-the-road area. We only had a couple more hours to go.

Suddenly everything was still. Deathly still. The squirrels quit chattering. There wasn't a bird in sight. The breeze had stopped. It was almost as if I were in a vacuum. My heart fluttered. The only time I'd felt the world this still was when I was in Minnesota as a kid. I'd been bucking hay bales into the barn on a scorching hot day. One minute the breeze fluttered the grass, the next everything in creation had stopped. I remember frowning at the sickly green cast to the sky. Then a cold breeze drifted over the field. Suddenly a horrendous rumbling like a freight train shook the earth and a tornado appeared out of nowhere. It plucked bales out of the field. I ran through the barn door just as a gust from the tornado sent me flying across the barn into the wall and then slammed the door shut. As quickly as it had touched down, it pulled back into the sky and disappeared.

I turned in the saddle, casting a glance to the west, the direction from which the storms usually came in this area. A towering mountain blocked most of my view. A sickly green tinge was oozing across the sky. *But we don't get tornados out here!* I thought.

My heart pounded as I fumbled with the buckles on my saddlebags. *If I can radio the ranger station, they'll be able to tell me what's going on.* My hands felt clammy as I fumbled out the radio and turned it on. I pushed in the button and held it close to my mouth. "Ondov to Seeley Lake." I glanced behind me. The whole western sky had now turned an odd green. No response. Only the sound of hoofbeats and Rye's panting pierced the silence. I pushed the button again. "Ondov to Seeley Lake." Anxiously I stared at the radio, but it was dead silent. Not even any static.

I took a bearing on the mountains that rimmed the valley. A peak stood in direct alignment between me and the repeater, which was the tower that was supposed to pick up my radio signal. Frantically I aimed my radio toward the repeater and pushed the button. "Ondov to Seeley Lake!" I waited. Silence.

Icy fear drained through my body. I was in a "dead zone," an area that didn't allow radio transmissions. I dropped the radio back into a saddlebag.

A frigid breeze rolled down the mountain. I kicked Czar into a fast walk, sweeping my gaze and looking for shelter.

Suddenly Czar planted his feet, his body taut, his head darting left and right as he looked around. I gathered my reins. "We're in trouble, boy."

It was literally the calm before the storm, and I was in the worst possible place. The charred-and-blackened spearlike tree skeletons stood 60 to 100 feet tall. They surrounded me as far as I could see. The fire had burned their roots so there wasn't anything to anchor them into place. A gentle breeze could topple thousands of these trees like toothpicks.

*What could a thundering wind do?* I wondered and then shuddered. I didn't want to be at the bottom of the pile.

*Where can I go?* I stood in my stirrups and looked. There wasn't a rocky outcropping or even a swale. We were in the middle of an enormous flat bench.

Czar's body quivered as thick, black clouds roiled over the top of the mountain. A gust of cold wind groped for my cowboy hat. I grabbed it and pulled it down tight. Drops of rain pelted us.

Czar pranced. *God, what should I do?* A tree cracked. I gripped the saddle with my knees. Czar threw up his head. One hundred feet behind me a tree toppled. Czar and Little Girl both spun and faced the pile, snorting and blowing. The tree squealed as it fell against another tree, knocking it over. Then another...and another, setting off a chain reaction. The whole stand crashed to the ground. Clouds of dirt and ash roiled up from where the trees smacked the earth.

Rain gushed from the sky. I fumbled with the saddle strings to untie my slicker.

Then I heard it—off in the distance. The sound of a freight train. I felt the blood drain out of my body. *No! A shear wind!* My mind raced through a memory of when I'd ridden through a section of forest that a shear wind had devastated. Uprooted trees blocked the trail. Huge branches hung suspended from the tops of other trees. But the scariest of all were the acres of stumps where trees had been sheared off a couple feet from the ground. The trees had simply vanished. They weren't anywhere to be found.

The rain fell in sheets. Charred trees fenced me in on all sides. I jumped to the ground and clawed my black slicker and jacket from the saddle. *I better put on as much padding as I can...just in case.*

Dust tornados mingled with rain whirled past and tugged at my cowboy hat. Czar and Little Girl milled around me, the whites of their eyes showing. I held tight to the reins and lead rope.

Rye whined and trotted in circles, looking for cover, but also wanting to stay with me.

Czar nodded his head and snorted at me.

The wind grabbed at my jacket as I tugged it on. I unrolled my slicker. The howling wind nearly ripped it from my hands. It lifted my cowboy hat. I slammed my hand against the hat and grabbed hold. The slicker beat me mercilessly as I tucked my cowboy hat next to my chest and snapped the slicker closed.

The rain fell so thickly I could only see a few hundred yards. It hit my cheeks so hard it stung. My hair was soaked, and cold water dribbled down my neck and back.

Czar butted me, trying to get me moving. My guts twisted as I looked around. All the trees waved with the wind. I snapped, "Where am I supposed to go?"

Dust mixed with rain pelted my eyes. A gust buffeted me. I swayed and leaned into it. My heart pounded.

The storm roared. Pebbles from the trail whipped me. The wind shifted and almost sucked me off my feet.

The air exploded. *Crack!* The tops of the charred spearlike trees snapped off. Suspended in a funnel, they twirled into the air. Then another air current snagged them and shot them past me like 50-foot-long arrows. I covered my head with my arms, but I was too terrified to close my eyes.

Drenched, I stood gawking in terror as row after row of trees tumbled to the ground all around me. The wind filled my slicker with air, threatening to lift me off the ground. Then it sucked the air out like I was a bellows.

Terror strangled me. My upper body whipped in the wind like a kite with no tail.

Something smacked my legs. Cold rain poured down my face as I looked down. Czar hid his head between my legs from the front. Rye lay between my boots and Little Girl had shoved her head between my legs from the back.

Both 1000-pound animals were trying to hide between my legs, along with a 125-pound dog. Then I did the strangest thing. I burst out laughing. "Hey, guys!" I screamed into the wind. "There's no room for me!"

The critters trusted me and had taken shelter in me. Tears mingled with rain washed my face, *God, I get it.* I looked into the heavens and shouted, "God, You are my shelter, and in You I will trust."

I can't explain what happened that moment. The clouds still boiled. The winds still raged. The trees still hurled past. But it was as if God had removed me from the storm, like I was now on the sidelines watching it happen. Fear drained away. Peace flooded in. I knew I'd be okay.

God was shielding me when there was no shelter in sight. I stood in awe and watched the sheer force of the gale subside.

As quickly as it came, the storm was gone. I stood dripping wet, staring at the tall stumps. Their tops were nowhere to be seen. Roots of the charred trees that had toppled reached like fingers into the sky. Rays of golden sunlight glittered across the forest floor. The violent storm had destroyed almost everything in this spot—except us.

I've never forgotten that shear wind. Now, years later, when I face danger or feel threatened, I remember that day and know that the God who lives inside me is more powerful than any storm I'll ever face.

*Lord, thank You for shielding me from the storms in my life and for being my security in this very insecure world. Amen.*

# 44

# The Radiance

*All around him was a glowing halo, like a rainbow*
*shining in the clouds on a rainy day. This was*
*what the glory of the LORD looked like to me.*

EZEKIEL 1:28 NLT

Cold raindrops dripped off the brim of my black cowboy hat and ran down the back of my black, oilskin slicker. The wispy September clouds oozed rain as I rode Czar down the trail that skirted the hillside above the canyon. Behind me trailed five soaking-wet mules loaded with packs, their hooves squishing through the mud. It was late afternoon, and we were headed into a camp in Dry Fork. The icy fingers of a light breeze tickled my neck. I pulled up my wool scarf to block it out.

Overhead the clouds churned, and the wind chased them. The sun poked through, dancing in beams across the trail as we dipped into a meadow. I turned to check the loads on the mules. My brown lead mule's packs rocked off-kilter, swinging heavy to the left side. "Aw, Little Girl, your packs rode so well until they got wet." I groaned. "And we're so close to camp." I reined Czar next to a tall pine and slipped out of the saddle. I tied Little Girl, with the string behind her, to the tree and then led Czar off the trail where I tied him.

Walking back toward Little Girl I glanced at the sky. I stopped. I'd never seen anything like it. Ribbons of glowing rainbows streamed across the sky. Not just one—multiple rainbows were stacked in rows of brilliant stripes. I'd seen as many as three rainbows nestled inside each other, but never spectrum after spectrum. I stood awestruck, staring into the heavens. The rainbows that rimmed the outside edges of the wide band merely blushed across the sky. The inside ones radiated dazzling colors. Vivid greens were bordered on either side by glimmering blues and shimmering yellows. The luminous reds faded into glinting violets.

There were so many rainbows I couldn't count them at a glance. I pointed my finger at the bottom edge and counted the green bands of color: 1...5...10...15...20...22. I blinked. "No way. There aren't 22 rainbows hooked together. That's impossible!"

Lowering my finger, I started counting all over from the bottom again. Yep, 22. I blinked hard and cocked my head. "No way."

Pointing my finger at the top of the rainbows, I counted the green bands while I dropped my finger toward the horizon. Still 22. "I've never heard of such a thing." I glanced around. *Is it because the canyon curls around the mountain and creates more reflections?*

My eyes were drawn back to the majesty of the rainbows that crowned the deep-green meadow. An interesting thought drifted through my mind: *Will it be like this when Jesus comes back? Will the skies declare His glory with radiant colors streaming behind Him?*

Slowly the colors washed out of the sky, but the memory has never faded. The radiance of the rainbows is permanently etched into my mind. I witnessed a piece of heaven visiting the earth with the glory of God. And I never would have seen it if those loads on Little Girl hadn't rocked off kilter.

*Lord, help me to see Your glory in my everyday life. Amen.*

# 45

# The Handshake Deal

*If you lend to those from whom you expect
repayment, what credit is that to you?*

LUKE 6:34

A light breeze whirled a dirt devil down the gravel road next to the campsite. I stood staring at the enormous pile of duffel bags and gear stacked on the mantie tarp. I had a few days off from my outfitting job, so my brother Chuck and I were heading into the mountains—just the two of us for four days. We'd leave in the morning as soon as he got off night shift. I'd brought the gear and arrived early so I could have everything ready. I rubbed my forehead. *We have enough supplies for a whole army! How am I going to get all this stuff on the mules?* I stared at the sleeping bags, tent, duffel bags, gas stove, kitchen boxes, tarps, and cooler.

A plume of dust roiled down the road. The ranch pickup flew past. It stopped at the orange blockade and turned around. Bill, my boss, drove next to me. He leaned out the window and tipped his cowboy hat. "It's sure nice that the road crew told us they were taking out the bridge and replacing it." He strummed his fingers against the steering wheel. "I've got horses and mules standing in a corral a mile behind that closure. How am I going to get across the river to feed them?"

I looked down at the North Fork of the Blackfoot River. Even though it was the first week of September, the water rushed over boulders. It was still too high to comfortably wade across.

Bill eyed my horses and mules that stood tied to the hitching rail switching their tails. "Would you mind if I borrowed one of your horses to cross the river and ride up there?"

I glanced at the horses and then at the pile of supplies. A thought slithered into my mind. "If you mantie my loads, I'll let you ride Melinda across."

Bill put a chew in his lip. "At the ranch I've got two trips worth of duffel to mantie, and I still have to catch some more stock. I don't know if I'll have time."

I lifted my shoulders and kicked the toe of my boot in the dirt. *Maybe I'm being stinky, but it'd sure solve getting my packs mantied.*

Bill glanced at the river.

Holding out my hand I asked, "Deal?"

He rolled his eyes and shook my hand. "Throw your stuff into the back of the truck. I'll take it to the ranch to mantie it and then bring it back in the morning."

The next morning I had the mules loaded when Chuck stepped out of his pickup. We slipped into our saddles and reined our horses down the trail. The sun had set behind the mountains by the time we pulled into a small grassy meadow with a few pines. Quickly I strung a high-line between two trees and tied the horses and mules.

Stumbling in the twilight, we worked furiously to unload the mules before the moonless night swallowed us. After digging the flashlights out of our saddlebags, I untied the ropes on the packs while Chuck set up the tent. We worked like a fire-bucket brigade. Holding the flashlight in my mouth, I tossed gear to Chuck, and he threw it into the tent. First our sleeping pads, then his sleeping bag, then…I dug through the pile. *Where's my sleeping bag?* I dug to the bottom. No sleeping bag. In the tent I heard Chuck pull his nylon sleeping bag out of the stuff sack. I waved the beam of my flashlight back and forth surveying the pile. "Hey, Chuck, did you grab my sleeping bag out of the pile?"

"No," he replied.

Frantically I dug through the gear again. I swept the ground with the flashlight beam in case the bag had rolled off the pile. "Chuck, I can't find it."

For the next 15 minutes Chuck and I cast beams of light through every bush and next to every tree. Nothing. Although Chuck offered me his sleeping bag, I refused.

I stomped over to the pile of saddles and pulled out the stinky and sweaty saddle pads. "I don't understand it. I gave that sleeping bag to Bill. Where could it be?"

Picking up a mantie tarp, I packed them over to the tent and made myself a cocoon out of the tarp and pads. I crawled inside. *Did Bill do this to me on purpose? No, he wouldn't do that. But maybe he should have. I was pretty rude. Why didn't I let him take Melinda without forcing him to mantie our stuff?*

In the morning Chuck and I searched for that sleeping bag, but it wasn't there. At night I snuggled in those stinky pads. By the end of the trip, I stunk like my attitude had been toward Bill—like a sour, sweaty mule.

A few days after we packed out, I stood in the ranch kitchen stirring a pot of beans when Bill drove the blue van filled with guests up to the gate. They unloaded, and he came up to the house and walked into the kitchen. He leaned against the counter. With a glint in his eye he asked, "Have a good trip?"

I nodded. "Did a lot of hunting," I said, pointing the wooden spoon at him, "for my sleeping bag!"

He rubbed his moustache, trying to cover his laugh. "When we got into camp and that sleeping bag was still sitting there—after all the guests had picked the duffel pile clean—I told them you were going to kill me. I'm sorry. I was so busy building loads for my two trips plus yours that I put that sleeping bag in the wrong load."

I burst out laughing. "Serves me right for holding you hostage. I'm sorry too."

*Lord, when I have the opportunity to do something for others, remind me to do it willingly instead of looking for how I will be repaid. Amen.*

# Tangled Up

*There will be no mercy for those who have not
shown mercy to others. But if you have been
merciful, God will be merciful when he judges you.*

JAMES 2:13 NLT

The fire inside the woodstove crackled and popped, sending waves of heat through the large canvas cook tent. Propane lanterns hung from hooks in the ridgepole, hissing loudly and casting golden glows throughout the tent. Hefting the large, blue enamelware coffeepot off the stove, I poured a steaming cup of coffee and handed it to Dave, a tired-looking crew member. He'd ridden the 14 miles from end-of-the-road camp with a string of mules loaded with hay. Tomorrow morning he'd pack the hunters out. I poured myself a cup and sat across the plank table from him. "How was your ride?" I asked.

He sipped the coffee and grinned. "Uneventful." He stuffed a cracker with cheese into his mouth. "Uneventful" was the cowboy code among us on crew that meant there hadn't been any wrecks with the pack string.

I wrapped my hands around the warm cup. "Did you drive by the main pasture and check on the horses?"

He chewed the mouthful and washed it down with coffee. "Everybody's fat and sassy on all that grass." Taking another bite he mumbled,

"When I was leaving, I noticed that Rahab was tangled in the barbed-wire fence."

My mind spun. Rahab was a filly born late this summer who had gotten mangled from barbed wire so badly that she'd almost died. We'd taken her over to Peggy and Howie's, the neighbors, and they had doctored her during the time we were in the hills. *And now she's tangled in barbed wire again?* I leaned forward. "And?"

He shrugged. "I untangled her." He stuffed another cracker into his mouth.

"Did she tear herself up?"

"Not bad." Cracker crumbs sifted out of his mouth as he swallowed.

I wanted to ask, "Not bad for a filly or not bad for a horse?" But he was totally unconcerned. *Did he even check her injuries? Or did he simply untangle her and walk away?* "What did she do after you untangled her?" I pressed.

"She lay down. I think she was tired from standing up."

Now I was so angry I was ready to blow. He didn't get it. I stood up and walked to the cookstove. "Was her mom around?"

He nonchalantly nodded his head. "She was with the herd, and they were in the middle of the field."

My heart pounded. I bit my tongue to hold back the anger. The field was nearly 400 acres! *Who could be so cruel as to leave an injured filly on the ground in coyote-infested country?* My heart ached for the little girl. She'd had such a rough life already and now this. *Did she have enough strength to get up and nurse off her mom? How long had she been standing in the fence?* The clattering hoofbeats of the hunters' horses drifted down the hill behind camp. After excusing himself, Dave walked out of the tent to unsaddle and feed the stock.

A million and one questions swirled through my head as I put the finishing touches on dinner. When the boss slipped through the door of the cook tent and hung his Elmer Fudd hat on a nail by the woodstove, I shared the story with him. He was as worried about the filly as I was. He chewed on his brown moustache. "It'd be good if somebody did ride out and check on her. But…"

I didn't let him finish figuring before I interrupted. "I'll go. You guys can manage bacon and eggs for breakfast." I twisted a dish towel in my hands. "Tonight, as soon as I finish dishes I'll ride out."

The wind moaned through the trees. Only a few stars hung in the black sky, and the moon hadn't risen yet. It was so black I couldn't see my hand in front of my face. Czar picked his way down the trail. I pulled up the collar on my winter jacket. *It's going to be another four hours before I can get to Rahab. Will she still be alive?*

The sound of water trickling over the waterfalls alerted me to the cliffs I was approaching. I shifted my weight to square up. Czar carefully placed his feet on the narrow trail that clung to the cliff above the falls. *How rotten of Dave to leave her there.* One of Czar's hooves dislodged a rock from the trail. As it clattered through the darkness, down the steep slope, and into the river, my thoughts fell into a pit. By the time I slid behind the steering wheel of the pickup and flipped on the headlights, I'd built a case of inhumane treatment and pinned it on Dave.

Headlights pierced the darkness as the truck rattled down the drive leading to the pasture. It was close to one o'clock when I hopped out and hung two halters over my shoulder. Switching on my flashlight, I paced to the gate. The barbed wire squealed in protest as I squeezed through.

With my flashlight I swept a path across the frosty field. Eyes glowed from the fence line. I waded through the waist deep grass. The mare stood next to Rahab, who lay shivering on the cold ground. Bending over her, I gently caressed her fluffy coat. Her skin felt cold and clammy. "Oh, little girl, let's get you warmed up." My thoughts seethed. *If I wouldn't have asked, the filly would have been dead by the time we rode out of the hills.*

I buckled a halter on the mare and then one on the colt. *I've got to get her into the barn, and she's too heavy to carry. Is she strong enough to walk?* Rahab's mom seemed to sense my urgency. She nuzzled the little one and nickered in low tones. The filly swung her head up and gathered her feet. Her front end lurched up and then she crumpled. Lying on her chest, she nodded her head and closed her eyes as if she were done in.

I stepped behind her, stomped my foot, and clapped my hands. "Get up!" Her head wavered. She was exhausted. From her nostrils, wisps of steam flowed into the crisp air. Focusing straight ahead, she inhaled and pushed her front hooves in front of her, stretching. Drawing them toward herself, she pushed with her hind legs. I caught her around the middle and pulled up as she struggled. Straining, I held her weight. Finally standing, she locked her legs and leaned against me.

Through the palms of my hands, I felt her heart pounding. "Good job, little girl. How long has it been since you ate dinner?" Instantly my heart soared. *If Dave wouldn't have been so cruel, you'd have a full belly and be warm instead of hanging on to life by a thread.*

Stretching, I grabbed the mare's lead rope and tugged it gently, guiding her next to us. As the filly leaned against the mare, the mare moved her hind leg back and nuzzled the filly's rear as if to say, "C'mon, kiddo, take a drink."

The filly reached underneath, weakly fumbling against the mare's udder. Finally she latched on and swallowed. In the dim beam from the flashlight I could see drops of milk roll out the corners of her mouth and drip off her whiskers. As the warm milk flowed into her belly, she slurped and butted the udder and sucked some more. Smacking her lips she turned and looked at me.

I grinned. "Tastes pretty good, doesn't it?" I encouraged.

The moon rose over the horizon, casting a pale-blue light over the field. I scooped up the flashlight, shut it off, and tucked it into my pocket. Stroking the filly's soft neck, I whispered, "God, please give me the strength to get Rahab to the barn so she doesn't die." Grasping the mare's lead rope, I tucked a loop of it under the left side of my belt. I knew I would need both hands to help the foal.

Moonlight streamed over the mountain so brightly that I could see my shadow on the ground. With my left hand I grasped the filly's lead rope under her chin and looped my right arm over her back and under her belly. Urging her forward, I tugged lightly on the lead rope and lifted her belly. She stepped and then leaned against me. Inches at a time we moved closer to the barn. With each step I bitterly pinned a new accusation against Dave. About halfway, I encouraged Rahab to nurse again.

The fresh smell of alfalfa hay greeted us as I guided her into the barn. She was so tired her nose was only a couple inches off the ground before she collapsed in the stall. I flipped on the light switch. The filly squinted. She lay on her chest with her black legs curled under her. Crouching next to her, I gently stroked her dingy-looking bay coat. I glanced over her body, looking for cuts and scratches. Dried blood caked several cuts on her legs, and she'd lost a fair amount of blood. The wounds were too old to be sutured. I seethed. *She should have gotten stitches earlier today.* As I doctored each cut, my heart oozed with condemnation aimed at Dave. *How can somebody be so cruel-hearted to a baby?*

I trudged up to the house, got ready for bed, set my alarm, and pulled up the covers. I drifted off to sleep with my thoughts hammering Dave. All night, every two hours, I got up and helped Rahab stand to nurse before tucking myself back into bed. After checking her in the morning, my boots crunched through the snow to the house. *What am I going to do? That filly isn't ready to be kicked out into the pasture, and we're all heading back into the hills the day after tomorrow.* With my boot I scuffed down to gravel. *I hate being a burden, but I have to call Peggy and see if they can take care of the filly again.* I sighed. *If Dave would have taken care of her right away, I wouldn't be in this fix.*

The heat from the woodstove rushed past me as I opened the cabin door. My leather boots thumped across the wooden floor as I moved to the phone and made the call. After hearing the story, Peggy offered to take care of the filly. My heart and mouth vomited accusations against Dave.

Peggy quietly replied, "Dave's not mean. I don't think he did it on purpose. He's just inexperienced."

I hung up the phone and felt like I'd been punched in the stomach. I had assumed Dave knew what he was doing, and that he had acted out of a mean spirit. Now I remembered that before he started working for the outfit, he hadn't worked with stock very much. Perhaps he'd never nurtured a sick animal. A thought flashed through my mind: *What if, when I first started working in the woods, people had assumed I knew as much as they did and judged me according to their level of expertise? I never would have measured up.* What Dave had done was not right, but my assumptions weren't either. The anger drained out of my heart and mercy flooded in.

The mare and the filly stayed at Peg and Howie's the rest of hunting season while Rahab healed up. I've never forgotten how harmful assumptions can be. They'd weighted me down with bitterness and anger. But a dose of mercy set me free.

*Lord, please give me the wisdom to be merciful to those around me. Amen.*

# 47

# Christmas Chorus

*My sheep listen to my voice; I know*
*them, and they follow me.*

JOHN 10:27 NLT

Snuggled in a blanket, I sat in my recliner sipping a steaming cup of morning coffee and reading my Bible. The rich scent of pine hung in the air. Only yesterday I'd driven up the mountain and cut a Charlie Brown Christmas tree. As soon as I drove in the driveway, I lugged it into the house, put it in the stand, and draped as many twinkle lights on it as the scrawny branches would hold. I yawned and stretched. From the pasture a long, drawn-out bray resounded, asking for breakfast.

I laughed. *Wind Dancer, I'll be out in a few minutes.* Setting my Bible on my lap, I glanced at the cluster of twinkle lights on the top of the tree while I marveled at the vastness of God's love. My eyes swept down the tree and then under the boughs to the pile of packages from family and friends. His love reflected from the bow on every present.

A deep nicker sounded from the pasture. I set the Bible on the end table and walked to the back door. *Dazzle, I'm coming. Be patient.* I slipped on my Carhartt coveralls, winter jacket, and Elmer Fudd hat. Opening the door into the snowy winter wonderland, I was greeted by a chorus of horses nickering and mules braying. Little Girl brayed and then honked at the end. With her low voice, Dazzle rumbled a nicker. Wind Dancer squeaked a bray. A long, chatty nicker came from SkySong, and Czar whispered his greetings under his breath. *God, I think it's so cool that You gave each of them a different-sounding voice.* I would recognize each one without seeing them. A thought rose up from my spirit: *You recognize My voice too.*

My mind drifted in amazement. *Yes, I do. But it amazes me that You, the Creator of the Universe, speak to me.*

After tossing hay into the feeders, I moved back into the house and cuddled up with God again. The lights on the tree twinkled, and peace warmed my spirit. *Yes, Lord. The greatest gift You gave was Jesus. Because of Him, there is no separation between us.*

*Lord, what a thrill it is to recognize Your voice. Amen.*

# 48

# Snagged!

*God will command his angels to
protect you wherever you go.*

PSALM 91:11 CEV

The digital alarm clock beeped. Punching snooze, I pulled my down comforter over my head and snuggled into the warmth of my flannel sheets. *Why is my bed always the perfect temperature when it's time to get up?* Usually when I punch the snooze button, I drift back to sleep, cherishing the added minutes. But this morning my eyes wouldn't close. I lay there staring into the dark. A thought bubbled up inside of me: *Why not say your prayers now?* I normally started praying when I headed out the door to feed the horses and mules and said amen after I got back in. Briefly I thought about the things I planned to do before I went to work. *I don't have time to stay here any longer. I've got to jump out of bed and get going.*

But that thought scratched inside me again. *Just rest and say your prayers now.* I sighed. *Why not?* I grinned. *That way I can stay in bed longer.* I rattled through my long list and finished with, "Lord, have Your angels protect all of us according to Psalm 91. In Jesus' name, amen." I had no clue that in a few minutes that prayer would determine if I lived or died.

I jumped out of bed and bundled up in my insulated Carhartt coveralls and pulled on my winter boots. As soon as I cracked the back door open, the horses whinnied and the mules brayed, begging for breakfast. I trudged through the dark to the barn and pulled out the sled I had loaded the night before with grain and hay. The critters followed me like dogs as I tossed flakes of hay into the feeders. Each time I stopped, I was careful to put the sled handle inside the sled so the animals wouldn't step on it and get tangled up. Out of caution, I'd made the handle out of twine so it would break if they did.

The snow glowed from the few stars that twinkled, and the moon had already gone to bed. The sled rumbled behind me as it scraped across the icy crust. I could hear Czar, my bay gelding, and Little Girl, my brown mule, slurping as they trailed behind me into the main pasture. They were both seniors, so I fed them extra goodies in a separate pasture to compensate for their rickety teeth and slower eating habits.

A coyote howled. Its song drifted over the low hills and faded away. This was my favorite time of the day. Czar and Little Girl's hooves squeaked in the snow as they trudged behind. I paused, letting Czar walk up beside me. I stroked his furry neck. "Do you realize how many decades we've shared our mornings together?" Czar had been my main saddle horse all the years I'd worked in the Bob Marshall Wilderness. He'd saved my life more than once. He leaned into my hand as I scratched his chest.

Little Girl nudged me, asking for scratches. I dug my fingers into the winter coat under her chin and scratched. I felt the knot on her jawbone where it had been broken when she was two days old. My mind drifted through the memories. The veterinarian had said her chance of survival had been almost zero, but I'd had him pin her jaw anyway. I bottle fed her every two hours around the clock—for months. She'd turned into the sweetest mule and didn't have a mean bone in her body. I dug my thumb deeper and rubbed. "We've been together a long time too, haven't we?" She lifted her head and shook it, making her long ears flop together. I giggled.

With the sled rattling behind, I strolled over to where the large, empty grain pans were in the snow. Stopping the sled next to Czar's, I dumped grain into his pan.

I groped in the dark for the handle and pulled the sled toward the other grain pan. I could barely see the outline of Little Girl's tall body as she followed alongside my left shoulder. Once again I carefully placed the handle into the sled, grabbed the grain bucket, and walked about five feet where I dumped it into her pan.

Slurping, she dropped her nose. She hunkered in to eat and moved her hind end one step sideways, placing her right hind foot into the sled. That one step started a chain of events that exploded so fast I didn't have time to respond.

The sled slipped backward under her weight. When she lost traction under her foot, it scared her and threw her off balance. She jerked her leg up, hooking the handle of the sled around her leg, which tugged the sled forward. In the dark, the sled rattled across the snow and slammed into her left hind leg. Feeling the twine tighten on her right foot and the impact of the sled against her left hind leg, she knew the bogeyman had grabbed her.

Instantly she reared up and pivoted 90 degrees to her right, slamming into me. I crumpled under her belly, and the side of my face smashed into the snow.

She stepped forward with her right hind leg—pinning my left leg to the ground. Feeling something under her foot, she lifted her leg. When she did, the rope from the sled, which was wrapped around her leg, looped around my leg. Now the rope tied to the sled was wound around her leg and my leg. In the pitch-black morning, the rodeo was on.

The tension on the twine cut into Little Girl's leg. She lifted her leg toward her belly, but the twine held fast. My extra weight on the twine must have felt like the bogeyman hanging on tight.

Little Girl snorted and jerked her leg up, trying to shuck the rope off. Instead, her raw power flung me like a ragdoll into her belly.

I tried to scream. The sound barely escaped my throat before I slammed into her belly and then thudded against the ground. All the air rushed out of my lungs. My hat flew off and rolled into the dark. Little Girl planted both hind feet to run away, and her right hind leg squished me.

The icy snow ripped at my face. Her front hooves danced around my head. I tried to cover my head with my arms, afraid she'd accidentally step on my head. As I lifted my arms, she whipped up her hind leg again, slamming me against her belly.

Although it lasted only seconds, it seemed like an eternity. Over and over she flung me against her belly and then I'd slam back to earth.

The hair on her front legs brushed against my face.

Her hooves thundered in the snow by my ears.

Suddenly the morning became deathly still. I lay in the snow; Little Girl was gone.

I spit snow and gravel out of my mouth, rolled to my side, and pulled off my mittens. Tracing my fingers over my face and head, I felt for lumps and warm blood. Nothing. I sat up and wiggled my shoulders and neck. *A little sore, but it doesn't feel like anything is broken.*

I stood up. My left calf ached, and my muscles felt like they'd been run over by a truck, but everything worked. I walked over to the sled. The twine was still in a loop; it hadn't broken. *Then why did it turn loose? It had all my weight against it, Little Girl's leg, and the sled. There wasn't any slack in that triangle of twisted tension. It never should have come loose.*

I bent over that sled, staring in awe. *That's why You nudged me to pray before I fed this morning, Lord.* My thoughts cleared. *The only way this rope could have gotten loose was for God's angels to have pulled it off.* God knew this was going to happen and had impressed on my spirit to pray before I got out of bed. I never dreamed there could be any danger with my old mule. She'd never done anything aggressive in her entire life.

My mind replayed the wreck—the hooves pinning me to the ground and dancing next to my face. *Did His angels cup my head in their hands?* I swallowed hard. God loved me enough to warn me ahead of time. But it had been my choice, my free will whether to pray. I could listen to Him or put Him off. *If I wouldn't have followed His leading to pray at that moment in time, I would have been severely injured or even killed.*

A loud snort broke the morning silence. It came from a hill 100 yards away. My heart sank. *Poor Little Girl. She probably thinks I attacked her.* She hadn't done anything wrong. She had been acting according to her instincts. She was a prey animal. Predators kill animals by grabbing them by their hind legs and hamstringing them or by jumping up and biting their bellies, ripping their guts out. Little Girl probably thought both happened when the twine wrapped around one hind leg and the other got slammed with the sled. And when she jerked her leg I slammed into her belly.

The snow crunched under my boots as I hobbled toward her. Little Girl stood quaking with fear. Nervously she shifted her weight. I stopped five feet from her and held out the back of my hand. In a low voice I said, "Bogeyman got you this morning, didn't he?"

She snorted as she smelled me. I stepped closer and touched her neck. She was as stiff as a board. I gently stroked her long winter hair. "I didn't team up with the bogeyman. I got caught in the middle."

She stared toward the sled and then glanced at me. I rubbed her forehead, and she leaned into my fingers. I chuckled. "I promise we won't do that one again. I'm not going to feed with the sled until I figure out a different handle."

After making sure she was okay, I headed back to the house. Stomping the snow off my boots, I opened the back door. I sat on the bench and peeled off my winter clothes, checking for battle scars. The muscles in my neck had gotten pulled, I had a mule hoof-shaped bruise on my left calf, and my back ached. Other than that, nothing was wrong with me. It was a miracle.

Later I made a trip to Missoula where my chiropractor worked on the kinks in my back. And for the next few days Little Girl kept me at a distance. She was sure I had something to do with all that drama. After a week, though, she gave up that thought and became my ol' teddy bear again.

I did get one battle scar that morning that has stayed with me. I learned the importance of immediately doing what God nudges me to do so He can take care of me.

*Thank You, Lord, for sending Your angels to guard and protect me. Amen.*

49

# The Big Red Bow

*If you give to others, you will be given a full
amount in return. It will be packed down, shaken
together, and spilling over into your lap. The way
you treat others is the way you will be treated.*

LUKE 6:38 CEV

The pines that lined the road sagged under the thick blanket of snow. The sun glittered off the snowy peaks, and the light breeze dislodged clumps of snow from the boughs. Plopping into the drifts through the forest, it created a drumming sound. A chickadee's whistle floated on the crisp air. I walked down the road leading Rahab, a four-month-old filly by my right side. Her mom was on my left. With every step their hooves squeaked through the snow.

It was the first week of December, and the outfitting season was done for the year. Yesterday the crew had finished packing the hunting camp out of the hills. I was looking forward to staying home the next couple of months after being in the wilderness all spring, summer, and fall. On the average, I had been in the mountains on trips 5 to 10 days in a row. Usually I only had two days between trips to drop guests at the airport, pick up new ones, and restock groceries before I rode back in.

I sighed and rubbed Rahab's neck with my mitten. "Now that the season's over, you can come live at home. You've been at Peggy's too long. How can we repay her for the two times she's taken care of you?"

Rahab had been born in late summer—not an ideal time frame for a colt to be born or to mesh with the outfitting schedule, but the boss had purchased her dam early in this summer while she was in foal. When Rahab was a couple months old, her nightmare began. She had charged the barbed-wire fence while trying to follow her mom, who had jumped over. The impact had slit the filly's chest wide open. I grimaced as I remembered the moment I saw the white bone of her shoulder exposed between bloody and mangled muscles. It was a miracle she'd lived. Because the whole outfitting crew was scheduled to work in the wilderness and Rahab required intensive medical care—dressing the wounds and giving her shots—my next-door neighbor and friend Peggy had cared for her. Because Rahab was still nursing, it meant her mom also stayed at Peggy's ranch.

I kicked a miniature clump of snow down the road. *How can I ever repay Peggy for the hours she and her daughters put into caring for Rahab? God, how can I say thank you?* I glanced at the healthy bay filly prancing at my side. "You're a miracle baby. You must weigh 300 pounds." The filly bobbed her head and danced sideways as we turned into my driveway.

Suddenly Rahab hauled back, ripping the lead rope out of my hand. She turned and raced down the road whinnying. I stood with my mouth gaping as she flew into Peggy's driveway and galloped into the barn.

*What is she doing?* I turned Rahab's mom around, and we clumped down the road to Peggy's barn. As I led the mare into the barn, the filly nickered at us. Catching up Rahab's lead rope, I stroked her fuzzy winter coat. "You are going to wear out your welcome here. It's time to head home."

I kept my eye on the filly until she settled into calmly walking by my side. My mind drifted back to the day I'd picked up Rahab last fall after her first bout with the barbed-wire fence. Peggy wouldn't take any money, and I understood. That was the "code of the West."

People helped out their neighbors without being paid. *But I want to do something for her. What can I do?* Lost in my thoughts, I relaxed my grip on the colt's rope.

Suddenly Rahab stopped and hauled back. I tightened my grip on the lead rope, but she squealed, reared up, and pivoted, jerking it out of my hands. Like a race horse, she flogged down the road kicking up snow from her hooves. Confused I stood there, wondering again, *What is she doing?*

Rahab barely slowed as she turned into Peggy's driveway and disappeared into the barn. I thought about having someone help me lead the filly, but Peggy and her husband, Howie, were at work and their girls were at school.

As I walked back to Peggy's barn with the mare by my side, my mind whirled. *Why would Rahab leave her mother?* I rounded the corner and entered the barn. Steam rose off the filly's back. Her nostrils flared as she panted. Grasping the lead rope in my mitten, I lectured the young horse, "You are being a real pain. Do you realize how much work you are for Peggy, Mary, and Jessi? They've got to clean your stall, keep your water thawed, and feed you twice a day. It's time for you to come home." I shortened up her lead rope and strolled out of the barn.

Steam puffed from the filly's nostrils as she pranced by my side. Memories drifted through my mind of the second time I'd asked Peggy and the girls to take care of Rahab. One of the wranglers had found her tangled in barbed wire. He'd gotten her out but didn't know anything about young stock. He'd left her there, and she'd nearly died because she didn't have the strength to stand and nurse. When I found out, I'd ridden out of the hills at night and found her shivering on the ground. If I would have waited until morning, she would have been dead. Once again Peggy stepped in. That was over a month ago.

At the end of the driveway I turned onto the road. This time Rahab planted all four feet and refused to budge. I wiggled the lead rope. The filly shook her head and backed up. I pleaded, "C'mon now." She widened her eyes until the whites showed, and then her whole body shook as she bellowed a whinny. She whipped up her head and pivoted. I braced against the rope. Her 300-pound body slammed the end. Her sheer momentum dragged me sideways and tore the rope out of my hands. Rahab raced to the barn, hollering the whole way.

Totally disgusted, I led Rahab's mom back into the barn. What I saw melted my heart. Rahab's body quaked with fear. She stood with her rear toward me, leaning her chest against "her" stall door. Fearfully she glanced over her shoulder, as if saying, "This is home. Don't try to take me away again."

Stepping alongside her, I rubbed my mitten across her back. "Okay, you can go back into your stall." I barely cracked the stall door open before Rahab charged through. Leading the mare in, I unbuckled their halters, closed up the barn, and walked home.

The heat from the woodstove rolled out the door as I walked into the cabin. Stomping the snow off my boots, I walked over to the phone and dialed Peggy. We chitchatted several minutes before I nervously laughed and said, "I couldn't get the filly home. She kept running back to your barn. She told me she was home."

There was a long pause. Then Peggy said, "I didn't want to tell you, but Jessi fell in love with Rahab. Jessi is the one who took care of her most of the time."

Winding the phone cord around my finger, I paused. It had been obvious, but I was so concerned about burdening them that I hadn't seen it. Rahab had fallen in love with Jessi. The filly's love for Peggy's daughter was so strong that she raced away from her own mom to stay with the person she loved.

My heart fluttered with the answer. *Horses are gifts from God wrapped in love and tied with His heartstrings as a bow—the perfect thank you.* I glanced at the flakes of snow on my boots that were melting and dripping onto the plank floor. "Peggy, what would you think about me giving Rahab to Jessi for Christmas?" I knew the boss would approve because Rahab couldn't handle strenuous mountain work due to her previous injuries.

Early in the morning, before the sun came up, I snuck into Rahab's stall and wrapped a wide red ribbon around her neck. I stuck a big red bow on the ribbon and then sat out of sight while I waited for Peggy, Howie, and the girls to come out to do chores.

In a few minutes, the large wooden door squeaked open and the lights were flipped on. Jessi skipped down the row of stalls to Rahab's and unhooked the latch. When she opened the stall door, I stepped into the light and said, "Merry Christmas, Jessi!"

Jessi looked at the big red bow around Rahab and then at me, as if asking, "Really?" Without pausing, she wrapped her arms around Rahab's neck and buried her nose in the fuzzy coat. Rahab closed her eyes, cherishing the hug.

That memory is etched in my mind as one of my most touching moments. It was so right that the person who gave freely of her love while expecting nothing in return received a bundle of love that day.

*Lord, open my eyes to opportunities to give things of value to those around me. Amen.*

50

# The Trail to El Shaddai

*Do you have a lonely nagging feeling that gnaws
at the very core of your being—like something is
missing, but you're not exactly sure what it is? Has the
excitement of life passed you by? Are you just going
through the motions, "serving time" until you die?*

Friend, I invite you to saddle up and ride with me on the trail to El Shaddai. The trail is filled with dreams and treasures of peace, hope, love, and wholeness. It's waiting for you.

You see, *El Shaddai* is a Hebrew name for God. Of all the names of God, this is my favorite because it can also be translated "The God of the mountains." It was during the 15 years I rode the craggy, narrow trails in the Rocky Mountains that I discovered how much God loved us—you and me—the people He created in His own image. Each of those days I experienced Him. His glory surrounded me from the sunrise glistening off the snowcapped peaks to the brilliant colors of gold, red, and purple splashed across the sky at sunset; from the cutthroat trout jumping in the streams to the eagles soaring on the wind currents; and from the frailty of a newborn fawn to the brute strength of the grizzly bear. God created it all for you and me to enjoy.

He even created you in your mother's womb with a very special plan and purpose in mind. He wants you to be a part of His family.

And that lonely feeling inside you is because He created you with an empty spot in your heart that only He can fill.

Some people tell me, "Yeah, that was then, but this is now. He wouldn't want me after what I've done." But being a Christian isn't about being "good enough" because nobody is or can be. It's by the supernatural grace and power of God that He forgives you and makes you acceptable to Him. It's about having a personal relationship with Jesus Christ. If you haven't accepted Jesus Christ as the Lord of your life, or if you've gone astray from Him, I encourage you to ask Him into your heart. According to Romans 10:9-10, "If you declare with your mouth, 'Jesus is Lord,' and believe in your heart that God raised him from the dead, you will be saved. For it is with your heart that you believe and are justified, and it is with your mouth that you profess your faith and are saved."

It's simple. All you have to do is believe and profess. You don't have to wait until you're perfect. Jesus died on the cross and was raised from the dead as payment for your sin. He died for you. Are you courageous enough to ask Him to forgive your sins and to come into your heart as your Lord and Savior? If so, from your heart, read this prayer aloud:

> *Lord, I am a sinner and cannot save myself. I believe Jesus Christ died on the cross for my sin. I believe He rose three days later from the dead so that I might have eternal life with Him. I'm asking You, Lord Jesus, to forgive me and to come into my heart and be my Savior. I ask You to live in me and to guide me from this day forward. Amen.*

Welcome to the family! Now it's important that you publicly express your belief by being baptized with water. Invest time each day with God by reading His Word—the Bible—and team up with other Christians so that you can share the journey.

May you be blessed with an awesome adventure on the trail to *El Shaddai!*

*Rebecca*

# Glossary

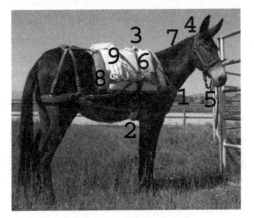

**Little Girl modeling gear**

1. Breast collar
2. Cinch
3. D-ring on packsaddle (front and back) used for sling rope
4. Halter
5. Lead rope
6. Packsaddle to tie loads onto animals
7. Mane (roached)
8. Saddlepad
9. Sling rope used to secure a load to a packsaddle

**Bay:** A horse or mule with a deep, reddish-brown coat and a black mane and tail.

**Breakaway:** A circular piece of rope attached to each packsaddle and used to tie the pack animals together, one after another. When an emergency arises and the rope is pulled hard, it's supposed to come undone or "break," freeing the animal.

**Breast collar:** A strap that buckles on the left side of the saddle, runs across the critter's chest, and buckles on the right side. It prevents the saddle from slipping back when the animal is traveling uphill.

**Bridle:** The headgear put on a horse or mule to provide control. The "headstall" part has an opening that goes behind and in front of the ears, with straps going down the sides of the animal's face to hold a bit (metal bar) in place in the horse's mouth. The bit rides behind the animal's teeth, so it is not uncomfortable. The reins are attached to the bit. When the reins are pulled back, the chin strap applies slight pressure to a nerve, getting the horse's attention.

**Buck:** When a critter has a temper-tantrum, he jumps up and down, back and forth, and any which way in abrupt motions to toss the rider or pack off his back. Sometimes horses kick up their heels in good-natured fun.

**Caulk:** A cleat attached to a horseshoe so the horse can dig into ice and not slip.

**Cinch:** A strap attached to the saddle on one side that is passed under the critter's belly and tied to the other side to hold the saddle or packsaddle tight to the animal's back.

**Coleman gas lantern:** A lantern that runs on white gas fuel.

**Colt:** A horse less than a year old. In general terms it refers to males or females, but specifically it means a young male horse.

**Critter:** Slang for horses and mules.

**Crupper:** An optional leather loop passed under a horse or mule's tail and buckled to a riding saddle or pack saddle to keep it securely in place, especially important when a horse or mule travels steep trails.

**D-ring:** A metal, D-shaped ring. On packsaddles it's used to tie on the ropes that hold the load in place.

**Duffel bag:** A cloth bag with handles for packing personal items, such as sleeping bags and clothing.

**Elmer Fudd hat:** Wool hat with a bill. Ear flaps are folded up inside. (See photo of Wind Dancer.)

**Farrier:** A person who takes care of horse and mule hooves by trimming and shoeing.

**Filly:** A female horse under a year old.

**Foal:** A male or female horse under a year old.

**Gelding:** A male horse that has been neutered.

**Halter:** Headgear for guiding a horse or mule. Made of leather, nylon webbing, or rope, it's used to control an animal when leading him or to tie him up so he stays within a particular area.

**Hitching rail:** Two posts driven into the ground with a horizontal post about waist high connecting them. A permanent tie-up place for holding critters in one place while brushing or saddling and when you want them nearby for later use.

**Hobble:** A wide leather strap that buckles together around a horse or mule's ankle. A picket rope is tied to it and a picket pin driven into the ground so the animal can move within a specific area to eat, drink, and rest.

**Hot shoe:** Fabricating metal shoes for a horse or mule using heat and bar stock or "keg" stock (pre-formed shoes). Using a forge to heat the metal, an anvil, and a hammer, a farrier creates shoes that perfectly conform to an animal's hooves. Hot shoeing requires more skill than cold shoeing, which is when a farrier uses a hammer and anvil to adjust pre-formed shoes.

**Kindling:** Logs that have been split into thin lengths; used for starting campfires.

**Lead rope:** A rope that attaches to a halter that is used for leading or tying up the animal.

**Load:** Whatever the critter is carrying on its packsaddle.

**Mantie:** Wrapping gear inside a heavyweight, white canvas tarp to create a compact load suitable for putting on a packsaddle.

**Mare:** A female horse.

**Mule:** A hybrid animal resulting from the breeding of a female horse and a male donkey. Most mules are sterile, although there have been rare cases of female mules reproducing when mated with horses or donkeys.

**Pack:** Gear wrapped in a mantie tarp that will be loaded onto a packsaddle.

**Packsaddle:** Specially designed saddle used for hauling equipment or supplies via an animal.

**Pack string:** Pack animals that have been tied together single file.

**Palomino:** A horse with a gold coat, although the color isn't always vibrant. The mane and tail are usually ivory or white.

**Pannier bags:** Large canvas bags used to transport gear. The bags have leather straps that buckle onto the D-rings of a pack saddle.

**Picket:** After placing a "picket pin" (a stake driven into the ground), one end of a "picket rope" (a rope ranging from 10 to 40 feet in length) is tied to the pin and the other is attached to a hobble placed on one of the front ankles of a horse or mule. This allows the animal to forage but limits its roaming range.

**Pulling string:** Leading pack animals that are tied together down the trail.

**Rear:** When a horse stands on its hind legs only.

**Roached:** A closely shaved mane.

**Rope corral:** Ropes strung between trees about waist high to form temporary pens to hold critters within a certain area.

**Sack out:** Training a horse to not get frightened by objects and noises by lightly flapping material around him and against his body.

**Saddlebags:** Two leather pockets or bags attached together that tie onto the back of a saddle with one bag on each side of the horse. Used for carrying small supplies and food.

**Saddle pad:** A blanket slightly bigger than a saddle, often with foam inside, placed under a saddle to provide cushioning for the animal. This makes the saddle more comfortable for the horse by eliminating chafing ("saddle sores").

**Slicker:** A raincoat.

**Sling rope:** A rope used to secure a load to the saddle. Applied properly, the sling rope enables a load to move just enough to make it comfortable for the pack animal.

**Sorrel:** A horse or mule with fur that is chestnut or light-reddish-brown in color.

**String:** Slang for a pack string of critters.

**White canvas wall tent:** Large tents made of heavy-duty canvas bleached white.

**Wickiup:** A small tarp tied between trees that is used for minimal weather protection for sleeping outdoors without setting up a tent.

**Wood cookstove:** A cooking stove fueled by wood.

**Wrangle:** Moving horses, cows, and other herd animals in a specific direction and to a specific location.

**Wrangler:** A person who works with horses or mules on a ranch.

# *Want More Adventure?*

Travel the trail again with Rebecca Ondov in
## HORSE TALES FROM HEAVEN!
*Also available in a beautiful, four-color gift edition.*

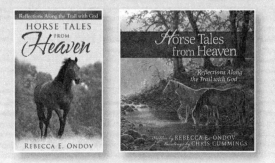

## Time to Hit the Trail!

Drawing on 15 years of living in the saddle while guiding pack trips and working as a wilderness ranger, gifted writer and avid horsewoman Rebecca Ondov invites you to experience life in a wilderness camp, discovering wisdom to live by through true stories about...

- a frisky cayuse and an early morning chase
- a night-blind horse and mule's unusual relationship
- a sleepless night in grizzly country
- a startling cure for snoring at base camp
- a wilderness "drive-thru" cafe

*Horse Tales from Heaven* captures authentic Western life and what it means to depend on God for love, provision, and grace as you ride the trail with Him every day.

To learn more about Harvest House books and
to read sample chapters, log on to our website:

**www.harvesthousepublishers.com**

HARVEST HOUSE PUBLISHERS

EUGENE, OREGON

For more information about Rebecca and her writing,
check out *www.RebeccaOndov.com*
or connect with her on Facebook.